Sami Sabet

Judge Me if You Can

novum ▲ pro

www.novum-publishing.co.uk

All rights of distribution, including via film, radio, and television, photomechanical reproduction, audio storage media, electronic data storage media, and the reprinting of portions of text, are reserved.

Printed in the European Union on environmentally friendly, chlorine- and acid-free paper.

© 2021 novum publishing

ISBN 978-3-99131-023-5
Editing: BA Hugo Chandler
Cover design: Engy Elboreini
Layout & typesetting:
novum publishing
Author's photo: Sami Sabet

www.novum-publishing.co.uk

I dedicate this book to my wife, who always believed in me and encouraged me to write. Also, a huge thanks to my daughter, Engy Elboreini, for the fantastic effort she put into designing the cover of this book.

Table of contents

"Who Am I?"

A day I can never forget, the one that signified the start of events that turned my life upside down: Monday the 17th of March 2008. I was sitting in my home office in shock, not knowing how this would end. Two men from Post Office Limited's (POL) investigations team were searching my desk, drawers, cupboards, and shelves for large amounts of cash or excessively high-value assets. They sifted through paperwork, looking for anything showing financial transactions, and placed objects into boxes as they deemed appropriate. Every so often, they came across a document to do with banks, or communications related to monetary transactions, and looked at each other before placing it in one of the boxes. Their expressions implied corroboration of wrongdoing and probable chastisement.

Looking around the room, I could not help noticing the lovely furniture, ornaments and paintings that adorned it. My gaze travelled out into the hallway, and I started to form a picture of our large, four-bedroom house, with three reception rooms and a big kitchen and breakfast room. Outside, at the back of the house, was a large, multileveled, decked garden with a very spacious art studio for my wife. My thoughts reminded me that, over the years, I had achieved a great deal, and become the envy of many. So, what led me to this predicament? Feeling frightened and very anxious, I found myself questioning who I really was, my past, work and social experiences, actions, and achievements. What had I done to get here? Would I be disgraced, humiliated, or worse? Did I deserve this?

Born in Egypt 53 years ago, I was the second child of what became a family of two parents and four children. My father, who was a dark-complexioned, always elegantly dressed man was born in Egypt. He graduated from Cairo University with a Medical degree and was intelligent and extremely sociable. During his post-graduation days, he worked as a gynaecologist, until he found his calling in Psychiatry. Actually, it was he who delivered my older brother, sister, and me. My mother was a young, beautiful, fair-skinned housewife who, like most women in Egypt in those days, had completed her high school diploma, but was persuaded not to continue her education. I believe, and indeed throughout the years she had proved, that she was more than capable in the field of finance and management, by the way she succeeded in the upbringing of four children and running our house. She instilled in us a kind, honest and caring attitude. Not only do I think she was the 'best mother,' but, also, an angel, putting everyone else's feelings and needs before hers.

At that time, we lived in a small flat, just around the corner from my paternal grandparents, in what was then an upper-middle-class suburb of Cairo. Their apartment was spread over two floors of a building and was huge, which is not surprising, as it housed a family of nine. There were two beautifully covered balconies overlooking the main road, approximately one mile away from the newly deposed king's palace.

My parents always thought that my sister brought luck with her. Very soon after Snats was born, my father secured a position as the first psychiatrist in Taif, Saudi Arabia. He had to travel there on his own to settle into his new job and arrange accommodation for us all to join him. Three months later, we were on our first-ever flight, heading from Cairo to a tiny airport in the coastal city of Jeddah. Along with one runway and apron, it had what looked like a large shed, built from corrugated steel sheets, as its terminal.

When we arrived, Dad was there to meet us. Our luggage was loaded into the back of a pickup truck, while we all sat in the front. He had brought this vehicle due to its luggage carrying capacity and its ability to endure the rough, very bumpy dirt road ahead. It was dark, but there was a full moon enabling me to see huge mountains around which we meandered. After a very long journey, we started to climb a mountain until we reached the plateau on which the city of Taif was built. Due to its high altitude, it enjoyed generally cooler temperatures than the rest of Saudi Arabia, a cleaner environment, and lots of greenery. The pleasant, inviting surrounds made it an ideal location for the king and royal family to spend the incredibly hot summers. Not only would they move to their residence there, the Government and administrative staff would also relocate their offices for the duration of the season.

We stopped in front of a large, detached bungalow, built on a substantial plot of land, enclosed by a brick wall; this would be our new home. As we got out of the truck, my father told Semita, my older brother, and I that he had a surprise waiting for us inside. Excited, we ran into the house to find an enormous room with a large rug in the middle of the floor. On two opposite corners were several toys for both of us. I was so thrilled I quickly forgot about the upheaval, the long and arduous trip and all that we had left behind. We were to spend the next few months in this house, which was divided into a private residential area for us, and a fully equipped medical clinic for my father.

Living there, I was very happy, playing with my toys inside and exploring new and adventurous activities in the garden. Once a week, my mother would go to the market and arrive back with about five men carrying huge wooden boxes of fruit and vegetables, and bags of general food supplies. One of the boxes, I remember, had prickly pears – shaped like a grenade, with thorns all over their thick skin. On the following afternoon, my mother, wearing gloves, had washed, peeled, and placed them on a tray and into the fridge. Later on, I opened it. There they were, piled in a huge bowl; reddish-brown, they appeared to be crying out for me to take. Delicious! One mouthful followed another and another until I had eaten half the contents of the bowl. I loved them and just could not stop, until Mum caught me. No more fruit for me on that day!

I saw many people arriving at my father's clinic. Some had companions and were driven there by drivers in big cars. They were wearing long white gowns (known in Arabic as a 'galabeya') and a scarf on their heads, held in place by what looked like a black rope joined to form a loop. One day, I was able to walk into the clinic without being seen and heard my father talking to his assistant in a room where the door was left ajar. Peeping in, I could see a man lying on a bed, with the assistant holding his legs and my father standing next to his head. In my father's hands were two small round probes, attached by wires to a machine. Around the patient's head was a band, under which the probes were positioned on either side of the head. He asked the assistant to hold the man tightly and flicked a switch while rotating a dial, making the needles move. The man's body and head turned violently, one way, and then the other. I was frightened, thinking that they may not want me to be watching this. So, I ran out before anyone could see me. I kept wondering why the man tossed and turned so violently. Did the probes on his head and in the machine have anything to do with it? Was he suffering? Much later on, I was informed that the man was a patient who was undertaking 'electric shock treatment.' Apparently, the electricity going through his brain was supposed to stimulate and return brain impulses to a stable state. That is, his brain is shocked into functioning properly. As I got much older and read more about the subject, I found this to have been, at best, a very simplistic view.

Although its exact mechanism or action is unknown, electroconvulsive therapy (ECT), as it is now known, is believed to treat difficult cases of depression or schizophrenia. It works by inducing seizure activity via electricity in the brain. The treatment lasts for a few minutes, carried out two or three times a week for a few weeks, followed by therapy on an outpatient basis. Although now frowned upon, it seems to have been used as recently as the early 2000s.

A year after moving into the bungalow, my parents decided to distance us from the clinic by relocating to a building, where our private residence occupied the first floor, with its own, separate entrance, leaving the ground floor for the new clinic. We spent three happy and eventful years there.

My parents made many friends, including some members of the Saudi royal family. Father's Egyptian colleagues were like us, with children of similar ages, and shared a need to feel close to the country they left behind, with its warmth and familiar culture. They would gather at our house, or we would visit them in their homes, and on weekends there would be outings to leisure parks where we would enjoy sumptuous picnics and BBQs.

On one occasion, my father took me to a lunch that he had been invited to by a prominent Saudi. They had prepared a feast at the centre of which was a large round serving dish filled with rice and topped with a whole grilled lamb. The table, with extremely short legs, was placed on the floor in a room which was open to the outside. Plates were placed around the table, as were cushions on which we would sit. Everyone sat around it crossed legged on the floor. However, my father could not do this, so they had to bring more cushions stacked up, enabling him to sit without having to cross his legs. Then came the interesting part! There was no cutlery, and I did not know how I should eat.

They pulled up their sleeves to their elbows, stretched their hands into the dish, grabbed a handful of rice, squashed it into a ball and put it in their mouths. In turn, they proceeded to hold the lamb with one hand while pulling a portion off by the other. They used only their hands to cut, mould and eat the food. It became clear to them that my father and I were not eating. We were not used to eating like this. The host asked the servants to find and bring a knife, fork and spoon for us. After the meal, I was allowed to explore the ornamental courtyard while the men talked and drank Arabic (Turkish) coffee and talked. Eventually we thanked our guest and took our leave. It was my first experience of lunch with company lacking in women, and men eating without utensils. Why exactly did they do this? I could not understand. However, I was informed that the proper way to eat like this was to use one's thumb and two index fingers to manipulate the food and place into your mouth. More importantly, you should do this using only your right hand.

At home, we had modern furniture, including a normal dining table with long legs, allowing chairs to be placed around, and be pushed, under it. We did not sit on floors. Mum had asked for a second, smaller dining table, with chairs, to be made shorter, especially for me and my brother. It was made to measure for our small sizes and heights, with appropriate chairs. We even had a 'child size' water jug, glasses, and cutlery.

There were several gatherings at our house, with friends being invited for lunches or dinners. They were fun, as we got to share our toys with other children. However, my birthdays were very special, when my parents held lavish parties. They included not only the usual feast of food and large birthday cakes, but also a cinema projector displaying the most recent films brought from Egypt. Mum spent days cooking and, with the help of a maid, arranged the seating to segregate men from women. The reason for this was because, in Saudi Arabia, men and women were not allowed to mix at social gatherings or business. If they had to meet, the women must remain covered from head to toe. This included their faces, which were hidden by a black veil, allowing only limited view for the women. To ensure comfort and freedom from such restrictions, they gathered, ate, and drank in different rooms. I used to wonder how the children knew who their mothers were. During the showing of the film, the women sat at the back, behind the men. When only our Egyptian friends were gathered, there was no segregation. Women dressed normally and mixed with men.

The princesses always brought the most sophisticated and expensive toys as presents. These included ones that were operated by batteries, which were very rare in those days. One of my favourites was a vehicle on wheels that responded to the sound of a whistle. When I whistled to it, it moved, whistle again and it stopped. At the same time, they always brought a similar, though more modest, gift for my brother and baby sister. Eventually we had a room full of these toys.

I had asked my father about what made these toys do what they did, and learned that they had magnets within them. One day, my brother and I were bored and decided to investigate. We raided the room, taking each toy in turn and dismantling it so that we may find out how they worked. We had destroyed 70% of these before our mother found us. After a severe telling off, we were banned from playing with the remaining ones for a month. We never managed to rebuild such a collection again.

Before long, it was the start of the school year. I was sent to a private kindergarten, and on the first day my mother accompanied me. There, I saw other children crying, as they had to leave their parents and forced to let go of their hands. I just went in and waved goodbye to my mum. Inside, toys were given to us to play with. Then, at midday, mattresses were laid on the floor and we were asked to lie down. They read us a story and after several minutes we were fast asleep.

Very early the following morning, a bus came to collect me from home. School was the same; play, being read to, and sleep. The school bus was there again after school and travelled around, dropping each pupil at his house. For some reason, I was the last one to be dropped off; by which time it was getting dark. My mother was furious as it was a very long day for me, and I had not been given anything to eat at school. She refused to let me go back again, despite my protests that I enjoyed my visits to the kindergarten. Alas, I was forced to accept what became the first of several, uncalled for and forced disappointments throughout my later life.

Two months before my 5th birthday, my parents decided to send me to a local primary school. The youngest in the class, I learned quickly, was able to communicate well, and was never frightened of questioning things. In so doing, I was instrumental in some changes in the school. One such change was the introduction of desks and chairs, allowing us to sit comfortably and not on the floor. One thing I did not question was the chalk, which we were given to write with on a small, A4 size, black writing slate.

Towards the end of the second term of the school year, the month of Ramadan started. During this time, all Muslims had to fast – refraining from food, drink and any impure thoughts or actions, from sunrise to sunset. On the first day, the school shut two hours early; pupils were collected or went home, and all the staff left. The gates were locked, and I was left alone outside. Within a few minutes I was standing on my own in an empty and silent street, with not a soul in sight.

Ali, a man from Yemen, was employed by my parents and tasked with, amongst many other things, taking me to, and collecting me from, school every day. He would take both my brother and I to our respective schools, which were not too far away from each other. Leaving home at about 7:30 in the morning, we walked to my brother's school, left him there, and then I would be taken to mine. At two in the afternoon, he would return to take me back home. As the school had closed earlier on that day, Ali was not there. I waited, feeling somewhat anxious, for what seemed to be an eternity.

All-of-a-sudden, walking up a perpendicular road to the one in which I stood, was a man carrying a large sack over his shoulder. The man approached the crossroads, and I imagined him coming over, grabbing me, and putting me into his bag. Filled with fear and panic, I quickly looked down the road to see if Ali was coming. Not only was he not, but there was no one else in sight. I decided to run across the road around the far end of a building, finding its entrance on the other side and hiding within it, under the staircase.

I was crying, felt sick and vomited. I tried to keep silent so that the man with the sack did not find me. After a long while, I stopped crying and started to realise that Ali would not be able to find me here and that I, cautiously, had to go back to the school in case he was there. Walking back around the building, I checked carefully that the sack man was not around and walked across the road to the school entrance. The street was still empty, and after some wait, I decided that I should do something, lest the man returned.

I remembered my brother's school was not too far and was confident that I could find it. Retracing our morning walk, I hesitated momentarily at a couple of junctions, deciding in which direction I should turn. After what seemed a long walk, I found it and felt happy that I was now safe with my brother. We would go home together when Ali came to collect him. However, as I approached the entrance, I realised that the school was empty, and my brother was nowhere to be found. Again, I was alone with no one in sight. I thought, "What do I do now?" Ali was not going to know where I was. I had to go back to my school.

Eventually, I arrived back and sat on the steps of my school building. After a while, I looked down the road and saw something. A long distance away, I could see a figure coming towards me. "Could it be Ali?" I dared not raise my hopes too high but kept looking intensely until he was close enough to be seen. By now, he was running, and I was sure it was him. I ran towards him and, seeing it was he, cried out, "Ali!" He opened his arms, into which I happily jumped. I was tearful but felt safe. At last, I was going home!

After a long walk in Ali's arms, we turned a corner to find our house diagonally opposite us. My mother was standing on the balcony, looking worried and tearful. Ali waved at her, shouting, "I found him!" Her face lit up with joy and she turned, starting to run downstairs to greet me. I wanted to jump out of Ali's arms and run to her, but he would not let me. Having crossed the wide, busy road, towards the building, he placed me in her stretched arms. She hugged me very tightly and kept on kissing me. It was one of the longest, warmest, most reassuring hugs I ever had. I felt safe again in her arms, but also proud that I did not allow the man with the sack to steal me.

Back in my office in Sussex, the POL investigators had finished their search and attracted my attention. They told me that they have gathered all the material they needed and would now like to carry out a recorded interrogation with me. I agreed, as I felt I had nothing to hide. They talked about the audits and discrepancies found and asked if I would be able to settle them by tomorrow. I could not, but I mentioned that POL had some £40,000, belonging to me, which, until now, had not been paid.

After an hour of questioning, they announced that they had finished and switched off the recording. They collected everything and left, informing me that they would be in contact soon. I sat down, reflecting on what had just happened and its possible implications. My thoughts returned me to the past, and Taif.

There, I was exposed to a great deal at a very young age. I recall on one occasion I was riding in a pickup truck, with a driver on one side and another man on the other. It is unclear as to why it happened like this, but they picked me up on the way to collect a man from somewhere. When they got there, they entered a house and several minutes later, came out holding a man who was shouting and struggling in an attempt to get loose. Looking through the back window, I saw them pick him up, throwing him into the back of the pickup and, using chains, tying his hands and legs to the four corners of the truck. I could see him stretched out trying to break the chains binding him, without success.

They came back into the cab and drove off, continuing our journey. I was quiet, thinking about what just happened and wondering why they had to chain him like this. Suddenly, I felt my underpants getting moist and asked the driver to stop as I needed a pee. As soon as we came to a standstill, the other guy opened the door allowing me to jump out, run behind the nearest bush and urinated. I felt really bad that I could not hold it and wanted to change; but where and how.

When we eventually got to the hospital where my father worked, I ran to his office and as soon as I saw him, started to tell him about what had happened. I asked him why they did this, to which he tried to explain that this should not be the case. He went on to tell me that the natives believed that people who reacted strangely, were possessed by the devil. They thought that they were keeping this devil under control and preventing him from taking the patient away. It was part of Dad's mission to educate and stop them from doing this. I never forgot the image of that patient, chained on the bed of the truck.

One day I joined family and friends on a drive, ending up out on the boundaries of the city. It was on the edge of the plateau, full of large rocks beyond which the ground seemed to disappear, appearing again at a distance far below. On these rocks were several baboons running and jumping freely. Although I was somewhat unsure, I did not feel threatened. People were throwing food to them, and I just stood there for some minutes, observing them, and wondering where they came from, where they slept or ate when we were not there. After several hours of a picnic and monkey play, we were ready to go home. In bed that night I thought that it would be nice having one as a pet.

A couple of weeks later, there was a knock on the door and a baby monkey was brought to us. Apparently, my father had mentioned how we liked them, and was given one. I could not believe my eyes and had to confirm that we could keep her. She stayed, and we called her Kerda. It was great for the first couple of days. However, it quickly became clear that we would not be able to control her, and my brother kept tying her up to stop her constant races around the house. My parents sadly decided she would get too big, mess up the house and would be uncontrollable; she could not stay. I woke up the next morning to find the house silent. Our Kerda had gone!

Several weeks later, we were taken, along with the normal group of friends, on yet another trip. We travelled to what seemed to be a barren land, depleted of any greenery. There were two concrete skeletons of buildings which, when completed, would form my father's new hospital, to be called "Amal", based on my mother's name, and our house. The villa, as they called it, was going to be enormous, made up of two floors surrounded by a very large garden.

The grown-ups left us to play while they surveyed the land and structures that had already started to form. We played, climbing onto the unfinished buildings and dirt mounds, had our pictures taken and had a picnic. My father had drawings of the buildings unfolded on a small table. The inside layout of the hospital showed it to be huge, comprising three stories and made up of three sections, forming a U shape whose sides had been pulled apart. There would be an area of plants, roses and trees all around it. The villa would have had four bedrooms with three bathrooms, three reception rooms, a kitchen and servants' quarters. It too was to have an enormous, walled garden surrounding it. We thoroughly enjoyed ourselves but, sadly, we never saw this project completed.

The Early Years

In 1962, my mother, brother, sister and I travelled to Egypt for what I had thought to be our annual holiday. However, it was earlier than usual, and my mother was pregnant. We stayed at my maternal grandparents' flat for about three weeks, then moved to a new one, a couple of miles away. It was on the seventh floor of a block situated on the corner of two main streets, opposite Heliopolis hospital. From our large, L-shaped balcony, we could see a good deal of the suburb Heliopolis. To the front was a very wide road with two carriageways for cars and buses, separated by pavements enclosing tracks on which the metro travelled. On the left side was an equally wide road divided by a tree-lined garden running along the length of it. Beneath us on our block were a grocer, fruit and vegetable shop and a couple of offices.

A few days before the end of May, my grandmother came to stay with us. Two days later, she took my mother to the hospital across the road from where we lived. On the first of June, my second brother, and youngest sibling, Sirkaak, arrived, and became the only sibling not to be delivered at home, and by my father.

A scuffle between Saudi Arabia and its neighbour, Yemen, had broken out. Egypt had sided with Yemen, resulting in tension between it and Saudi. Despite this fallout, the Saudis asked my father to stay, offering him citizenship and the position of Minister of Health. He felt strongly about the situation and the unfairness of the Saudi Government towards the Yemeni people. His strong beliefs forced him to reject the offer and resign.

Three months later, he gathered our belongings and returned to Cairo for good.

My mother had to hire a maid to help her with household duties and look after my baby brother and sister. Semita, my older brother, and I were both sent to the local Primary School, about half a mile away, on the same side of the road as our flat. We had returned to a much busier, more cosmopolitan environment to that of Taif. Our 8-storey block of flats, along with the shops underneath, dwarfed any building in Saudi, and the metro line, which covered the whole of the Heliopolis suburb, was only one of many all over Cairo.

Our neighbourhood was fairly new, with several blocks of flats being built further to the east of us. These numerous building sites offered brilliant opportunities for me to explore. Apart from the metro and buses, there were very few cars on the street, though it might not have appeared as such compared to Taif, due to the enormity of Cairo.

When we were in Saudi Arabia, I was very fond of Ali, who took good care of me and played with us. When we left, I was startled that he had bought me a pen as a present and nothing for my siblings. I guess this fond memory of him drew me to the builders and security guards working on the building sites. Some of them displayed his mannerisms and had similar accents, encouraging me to visit, talk and drink tea with them. They told me stories about where they came from, the families they left behind, and how they lived. Most of them had come from Upper Egypt to find work, as there were no jobs in their villages, and they needed to make a living. They had to leave their wives and children back home, because they could not afford to bring them to Cairo, or because the children were at school and could not relocate. Living on site and working every day, they barely spent any money in Cairo, sending it to their families back home instead.

At school, I made a lot of friends and enjoyed many adventures, challenges, and a great deal of fun. I liked my teachers and felt that they appreciated my hard work and ability to acquire and assimilate information quickly. Although the school was within walking distance from home, we enjoyed riding on the metro. Neither myself, my brother, nor my friends were given money to buy a ticket. Instead, we would jump on the back bumper of the train, hang on for dear life, and get off at the stop opposite the school. More often, however, we would get into a carriage and, when the conductor approached, we would move away from him, until the nearest stop, where we would jump off. It was great fun, although it was for a very short distance. On our return from school, we walked, talked and frolicked with our friends.

On some evenings and during weekends, we would be taken to my maternal grandparents' flat to stay. My grandfather, a short, stocky man with glasses, was a headmaster of a large, well respected private school. My grandmother, who was taller, did not work and spent a great deal of time with us. I loved being with them in their massive flat with, at the front, an office with a guest reception room and balcony on one side, and their bedroom and another balcony on the other. In the middle section was a large reception room connecting these rooms, together with a big dining room and a wide, long, corridor, which in turn led to a kitchen, cloakroom, two further bedrooms and a bathroom. One of the bedrooms had its own balcony, whilst the other had two – one on either side. It was the only flat on the fourth floor of the building.

I used to walk around, admiring all the antique furniture and ornaments in the reception areas. An archway separated the lounge and dining room. Net curtains, acting as a partition, gave me a mysterious anticipation when walking from one room into the other. I loved the brass and, even more so, the bronze ornaments. One of my favourites was of a man standing in a chariot, holding a raised whip with his right hand and, in his left, the reins, connected to two horses with heads held high, appearing to be charging at speed. The whole sculpture was mounted on a rectangular, solid piece of marble, measuring approximately 50cm by 30cm.

One item, which made a huge and lasting impression on me, was a grandfather clock. It rested against a wall halfway down the corridor. I used to sleep in the room on the other side of that wall, and could hear its 'tick-tock' sounds and chimes all night. It had become a comforting sound, which has stayed with me throughout all these years.

One day in May 1963, we were at the flat with other members of the family. My grandmother was in bed, though it was in the afternoon, and members of the family were standing in groups, talking to each other. I went into the study and heard my father speaking to my grandfather and a couple of other aunts and uncles. He said something like, "I am afraid there is nothing that can be done...it could be a matter of minutes..."

The women started screaming and hurriedly walked into my grandmother's room. As they stood around the bed, I walked to the bottom of it and stood there, at her feet. Looking around, trying to understand what was happening, I saw my mother and aunt standing next to her, with my father's sisters and mother on the other side. She was lying on her back with her eyes closed and everyone looked sad and tearful. People would come into the bedroom, look at her and, with a sorrowful expression, walk out again. I thought, "Why, with all this noise around her, did she not wake up and open her eyes?" It felt as if something was wrong and that I had to stay to see what would happen.

With all the commotion, no one noticed me. After what seemed a long while, my grandmother started to toss and turn in bed, as if having a seizure. She seemed to be trying to get loose, like the man I saw, chained on the back of the truck in Saudi. Suddenly, she became still, and her mouth dropped open. Everyone started crying and, some, screaming. My mother and aunt bent over her and hugged and kissed her. They were crying uncontrollably, while the others, also, crying, walked over to console them. I touched her exposed feet and found them cold and hard. Someone got a large scarf and wrapped it around her chin and head to force her mouth shut. Then, they pulled the cover over her face and head. They then realised that I was there, and quickly ushered me out of the room.

I remember wondering why I was unable to cry like them but felt that I wanted to memorise this moment. The day was

Thursday 16th of May. I walked to my favourite clock and heard it chime six times; it was six o'clock in the evening. I sensed that this was bad and knew I would never see her again. Funnily, for some reason, I remembered the rose petal jam and butter sandwiches she used to give me for supper; I loved them and continue to look for and enjoy them even now. I would never forget the moment I last saw my adorable, kind, and elegant grandmother.

We spent the following three days at her house. On the following morning, wrapped in a white sheet, looking just like a sweet with its wrapping twisted at either end, my grandmother was taken out of the house. Semita, Snats, Sirkaak and I were not allowed to attend her burial. However, over the following three days, members of the family and friends came to pay their respects and offer their condolences. Waiters were walking around offering mourners Turkish coffee and water. The radio was on, broadcasting verses from the Koran to do with a person's death and expectations of Heaven thereafter. After this period, we were taken home, and back to normal life.

My father decided he would open a private clinic in central Cairo, where most clinics were found. He eventually found one in a road called Sharie Sherieff, similar to Harley Street in London. Along with this, he also decided we should move nearer to his work and the centre of the city.

We moved into the elite island on the river Nile, called Zamalek, which was connected to the mainland by four bridges, two into town on the east side and two to the west. The building in which the new flat existed was only two stories high, sharing the wall enclosing the Officers' Club on its west side. Our flat was of average size, comprising one huge master bedroom, a very large second bedroom, a bathroom, cloakroom, large kitchen-breakfast room and three reception rooms, each of similar sizes to the master bedroom. In the dining room was a rectangular dining table with eight chairs, of which two were carvers, and a sideboard storing plates, glasses, and cutlery. The room was so big, I used to ride my bike around it and, on its dining table, play ping pong with my brother and friends. There were three balconies and, through the kitchen-breakfast room, more access to the outside through what was called the servants' staircase. We used it to climb to the roof, play and, when organised, watch a famous singer, Om Kalthum, perform in front of the president and other senior officers, on stage in the neighbouring club.

My brother and I went to the local government school, whilst my sister found herself in a private preschool called 'Baby Home.' We also joined the very exclusive Gezira Sporting Club, set in approximately 400,000 square metres of land, housing an outdoor cinema, six swimming pools, two football pitches, two gyms, basketball, volleyball, tennis and squash courts. It also housed restaurants and cafes, various activity areas, croquet lawns, a nine-hole golf course, and a horseracing track with large stand and stables. It was magnificent and the most exclusive club in Egypt at that time.

At school, I was always first or second in class, captain of the basketball team, and helped run the student social club, where we played board games, backgammon, chess, and many other games. We also set up groups to discuss or debate any topics we felt inclined to explore. Every day, before classes, the whole school attended a morning assembly outside in the playground. Everyone would stand in line, along with their classmates, while the headmaster would greet us and speak about forthcoming events during the day and other topics.

One day, he introduced a teacher who was going to lead us in performing some physical activities. He started by showing us how to do the first one. In my eagerness, and wanting to do it well when asked, I practised it. I was only 10 years old. He saw me and promptly asked me to join him at the front. With a very loud, aggressive tone, I was asked if I had heard him give the order to start the exercise. I replied, sorrowfully, that I had not and apologised. To my surprise, he asked me to hold the palm of my hand out and proceeded to hit it with a cane. I was in shock and pain.

This had never happened to me before, as I was always well behaved in class and completed all the tasks asked of me. Whenever there was misbehaviour, and the teacher could not find out who was responsible, he would cane everyone except me. Instead, when he approached me, he would ask me to sit down, without punishment, knowing that I would never break a rule. As far as I was concerned, on that day, I had not done anything that deserved such punishment. Apart from the pain, I felt embarrassed and humiliated in front of all my friends, teachers, and the whole school. Everyone seemed surprised and gasped as I was dealt the blows. I detested him and had no intention of carrying out his stupid instructions. Staring at him, desperately holding back tears, I turned and walked away quickly to my classroom.

A couple of weeks later, I fell ill with a fever. My mother informed the school, and, for the first time, I had to stay home. I missed my friends and the activities we normally enjoyed. After school, to my mother's surprise, almost the entire year came to ask about me. They had to wait, as mum did not want them to be infected – and, of course, there was no room for them all! I was told to look outside our balcony on the first floor. I could not believe what I saw. At least 60 pupils, standing in three rows, were waving and shouting, "May you get well soon!" I thanked them and we had a few conversations about what they did at school, how the club did not open, and several other interesting happenings. My mother told me that the time had come when I must go inside to rest. So, I thanked everyone and waved them goodbye. I felt better for seeing them, and also appreciated the effort they had gone to, just to come and ask about me.

On Thursdays, Semita and I, along with two other friends, would take our bikes out and ride around the area. We would explore new places, initially on the somewhat large island on which we lived before we expanded our routes to include suburbs further afield. It was fantastic and very informative. We rode through much poorer areas with dilapidated houses, dirt roads, and green fields beyond, where we discovered a local small airport with a lot of private, single-engine planes flying into and out of it. We learned a great deal about aeroplane technical details, about flying and the use of wings and rudders, as well as the type of fuel they use.

This proved very useful, as, sometime later, my cousin Tutu came to visit and brought with him a petrol-driven, remote-controlled plane. It was empty and he was not sure if he could buy normal fuel for it, from the local petrol station. I told him about the airport and the fact that, probably, he would need a special aviation fuel, which was found there. My brother and I took him there and managed to purchase the fuel. We filled the plane and took it to a large field nearby. There, we were able to fly it and spent a couple of hours taking turns to do so. It was a great experience making this plane fly at differing heights, turn in the air and land. I felt like I had become a pilot and, indeed, thought that I wanted to become one when I got older.

One Thursday, we decided to venture further out than normal and rode our bikes towards the Pyramids of Giza. After riding for three hours, we began to see the largest one, Khofo, in the distance. However, we realised it was getting late and turned back. By the time we got home it was dark and my mother was there, waiting for us. With her arms crossed, she looked very angry and started to shout at us, demanding to know where we had been and why we were so late. We tried to explain that we did not mean to. However, she had the last word. Our bikes were to be locked in a cupboard for three weeks; we would not be allowed to ride them. It was final and there was nothing we could say or do to change this.

As we were members of this brilliant Gezira Club, we went there whenever we were not at school. This was mainly on Fridays, and during some afternoons and school holidays. A couple of our friends were not members and we always had to find a way to smuggle them in. Once there, we would go to the kids' garden and play marbles. There were many different types of plays, all resulting in winning or losing marbles. Some people would set up their marbles in different designs – in a straight line, forming a triangle, or other shapes, containing from two to six pieces. They would draw a line, about three to five metres away, behind which punters would stand. The idea was to hit the set-up marbles by throwing or rolling your marble at them; a bit like bowling, or the French game, Pétanque. Some marbles were bigger, and others more colourfully decorated, rendering them more valuable. Over the months we became experts and had accumulated a number of these exquisite ones. Over time, I had enough marbles allowing me to control the games and have others trying to win my collection. I was lucky in that I won more marbles than I lost.

I had not been taught to swim but felt that I wanted to be in the deep, Olympic sized pool. Through watching other people swimming and learning from books, I decided to teach myself. In the shallow end of the pool, I went down the steps and stood in the water in the corner with one hand holding the side and the other holding the adjacent side. I raised one arm over my head, bringing it down, reaching for the other side. I continued to increase the distances, and number of strokes needed, until after several practices I was able to perform the front crawl, swimming the width of the pool. Further observations of other swimmers and reading swimming instruction books taught me the correct techniques.

Later, I decided to join the swimming and diving clubs and received professional training. During the spring and summer holidays, I used to visit the club every morning for practice and more advanced training. Not only could I swim fast and over a very long distance, but I could also dive from three-metre springboards as well as five- and ten-metre platforms. I was able to dive backwards and perform somersaults and twists from all levels. Unfortunately, I did not get the chance to continue this to national competitions, as my parents kept taking us away to the coastal towns of Port Said and Alexandria for holidays lasting two of the three summer months.

I loved my life in Egypt. Along with many friends, there were many activities to enjoy, within the club, school and around town. My grandfather would come to visit us once every two weeks and give my siblings and I ten piasters each. They would buy sweets with their money, whereas I would buy fruit, like watermelon, mangos, figs and prickly pears, for the whole family.

I occasionally bought the odd bar of chocolate for myself, with spare cash. Sometimes, I would treat my friends, or the porter's children, offering them drinks, or confectionary. It made me happy to see everyone enjoying themselves.

I used to collect Snats from her school and take her around the island on the bar running from underneath the seat to the front handlebars of my bike before heading home. Visiting our relatives in Heliopolis (a suburb of Cairo, about 10 kilometres from where we lived) was a real treat and thoroughly adventurous. Life was indeed good then.

The West
A New Language And Way Of Life

In 1966, my father was offered a position as a psychiatrist in the United States of America. It had only been four years since our return from Saudi and I had started to settle into our new way of life. Though large, the city was safe, with few motor vehicles, clean roads, and large green parks and flowerpots along the central reservations. Our life, socially, academically, and physically was, as far as I was concerned, perfect. My headmaster pleaded with my father to leave me there, at school. He argued that he found me to be very bright, with excellent potential, which would not be realised due to the different systems and language to which I would be subjected. My parents could not leave me behind and were sure that I would adapt quickly and succeed. There was no escaping yet another move; only this time, it would be more severe, with a major change in language, education, and way of life. The decision was taken, the house prepared for a period of emptiness, and we were on our way.

The long but exciting journey started with family members taking us to the airport. We flew to London on board BOAC, with a layover there, followed by another flight to New York. A further taxi ride and we were at a hotel, fairly nearby. The following morning, my father took us out for breakfast in a typical American diner. I had a couple of fried eggs, sunny side up, as they called it, streaky bacon, a couple of pieces of toast and a large, sugared glass of milk. This was the first time I had such a breakfast and I loved it. Later on in the day, we returned to the airport and caught a flight to Louisville, followed by a drive to

Lexington, in the state of Kentucky (known as the 'Blue Grass State'). I did not know any English and was reliant on my father to translate everything for me. The roads were smooth, lined and clean, with nicely maintained pavements, or 'sidewalks,' as the Americans called them. There were minimal blocks of flats and tall buildings, and most houses were a maximum of two storeys, surrounded by green land.

Father had been given a house on the hospital grounds in which he worked. For the first couple of months, I would play with the local children, communicating using sign language and various expressions. However, I knew I had to properly learn not only English words, but, also, the phrases and order in which they were used to interact and express myself well. Watching a lot of television helped a great deal with learning and pronunciation. I was happy. Amongst other things, I was intrigued by a vending machine, which dispensed carbonated beverages in glass bottles. I placed a coin in a slot, opened a small glass door of a compartment and took the drink I chose. On the side of the machine was a bottle opener with a box underneath it to collect the tops. Whilst residing on the hospital grounds, we were expected to use the staff canteen for breakfast lunch and dinner. I loved the cereals in the mornings, the mashed sweet potatoes, and the chocolate milk, served in small cartons shaped like a house. Things were certainly different from Egypt.

Our stay on the hospital grounds came to an end after three months, when we moved into a house in one of the suburbs. It was a charming bungalow with a big garden that was extremely different from the flat in which we lived in Cairo. I was enrolled at the local elementary/junior school, where I was immersed further into the language. Using all the resources I had, including my favourite book, Pictionary, TV, friends, and neighbours, I quickly learned how to speak, read, and write. By the end of the school year, I had become sufficiently fluent to allow progress into secondary school, or junior high, as it was known.

We moved again, within Lexington. This time the house we moved into was a two-storey, much bigger, detached one. The street on which we lived formed a large square with enormous Oak trees lining both sides of its road. North Arcadia Park was to be one of the nicest areas in which I lived. Our neighbours came round and introduced themselves to us. The local paper wrote an article about us, including what my father and mother did and where we came from. They too welcomed us to the city and wished us all the best. Everyone made us feel very welcome.

Every morning, my brother and I were collected by a yellow school bus with a stop sign on the side, which opened to warn cars that it was stopping and that children would either be climbing on or getting off. Basically, this was like a 'lollipop' person (so named by the stop sign with a handle, carried by them and resembling a lollipop) in the UK, stopping traffic, to allow school kids to cross. It would stop just outside our house, take us to Southern Junior High School and return us home in the afternoon. I enjoyed school and, academically, was performing well. Socially, I was popular, and, during school dances, was never short of a partner to dance with. At the end of the year, we would be given the school's yearbook, where all our pictures were included. Two pages at the back were left blank for fellow students and staff to write their greetings or comments. I always had many very encouraging comments, making me feel wanted, cared for, and like I belonged.

I discovered that I must have had entrepreneurial tendencies. Around the Christmas season, I decided to buy boxes of Christmas cards, in bulk, and walk from door to door, selling them. In the summer, my parents tasked me with mowing the lawn and bought a petrol-operated mower to help me achieve it. After I finished mowing our lawn, I thought that others may want to do theirs, but may not have had a mower, or did not want to put in the effort. This belief led me to calling on my neighbours and asking them if I could do theirs. I charged them $2 for an average size garden, and very quickly had enough work to keep me occupied for the whole of the season.

One of my clients, Mrs Gum, liked what I did and asked me if I would be interested in learning gardening. She must have been in her late fifties and had a large house and plot of land, two minutes walk from my home. I was allocated a patch of land big enough to plant several different vegetables, supplied with the necessary seeds and shown how to prepare the soil and use the appropriate tools. One or two days a week were spent planting things like runner beans, cucumbers, tomatoes and others, and enjoying it immensely. After several months, I asked her about the seeds we used and expressed my interest in purchasing and selling them to other gardeners. Again, she encouraged me and reminded me of the Christmas cards I sold earlier. She showed me where to buy them, and, when they arrived, I was made to pretend that she was a potential customer and go through the sales process, with her pointing out actions which would not be helpful and forcing me to practice what to say and how to speak to maximise sales.

Socially, I made a lot of friends around the neighbourhood. Danny was one of my best friends. We both had small, four-wheeled wagons that accompanied us everywhere during our free time together. Our heavy toys and other things were transported between our houses and when going on outings. When Mum sent me to the local store to buy something, my wagon would be with me to carry the stuff back.

During the autumn, the leaves from the giant oak trees lining the road would cover the ground. They would be gathered along the pavement, waiting for collection by the council when they became too much. I remember my friends and I used to lie down by the pavements and cover ourselves with the leaves. I can't imagine what would have happened had a car decided to park where we were hidden!

One day, I was playing with a couple of friends, one of whom had a Go-Cart. Gary showed me how to start, stop and drive it and, having demonstrated driving it himself, let me have a go. It was great! I started it by pulling a cord, as instructed, got on it, hands on the steering wheel, activated it and, with a press on the pedal, was off. I drove slowly at first, in a circle, then, when I became more confident, sped up. On one of the runs, I quickly started to run out of road, approaching a T-junction with the busy main street. I pressed the brakes and nothing happened; I tried several times, and the cart would not stop. My friends shouted "Stop, stop!" forcing me to shout back, "It won't stop!" They mentioned spark plug and I started to panic. The main road, with cars flowing through it, was getting very close. Then I realised what they had been trying to tell me, turned around and saw the spark plug with a piece of metal over it. I quickly pushed the metal down on the plug, and the motor cut out. I stopped just at the junction. Phew! I must remember to always check the brakes before riding a go-cart again!

We spent three years in America, and I cannot remember a day when I felt different, unwanted, nor told anything that could have been construed as racially motivated or felt any disharmony. Sadly, however, due to visa rules, we had to leave and reapply for a different visa before we could move back. We flew to Libya in North Africa, west of Egypt, where we stayed for just over a year, before, as my father originally thought, we could apply for the 'immigration visa' to get us back to America.

We landed in Benghazi, where my father had been given a position as a psychiatrist, with a contract lasting one year. When he went to take up his post, the terms and conditions had been changed. They informed him that, because he was Egyptian, they would only pay him half of the contracted salary and a much-reduced housing allowance. He had been working in America as a psychiatrist and had acquired their qualifications, verifying his educational standard, gained several years of training and experience and was, by then, a highly qualified, sought after psychiatrist. Added to this, he was multilingual, being fluent in both English and Arabic. To add insult to injury, he discovered that a British colleague, with less experience than him, was paid double the salary and given much better housing allowances. He also had an Arabic-speaking assistant to translate what the patients were saying and what he wanted to say to them. Needless to say, my father could not accept this.

He voiced his disappointment and disgust at their changing of his terms after he had got there and informed them that he would not stay. A couple of days later, they had changed their minds and offered him equivalent remuneration and benefits. I was just under fourteen years old and could not understand why there should be such discrimination, and how can anyone change an agreement after allowing the person to leave his or her job, home and, along with his wife and four children, travel thousands of miles.

A few weeks later, on September 1st, 1969, I woke up to the sound of gunfire coming from outside. The radio was broadcasting military music and saying something about a revolution. I went out into the balcony and found the streets full of soldiers carrying rifles and shooting in the air. The King had been ousted and Colonel Gaddafi took his place as the president of the country. They bragged that it was a bloodless coup, ridding the people of the tyranny and repression of the King.

Before that day, everything in the country was clean, well maintained and elegant. Cinemas were furnished with leather, wide and comfortable, armchairs. Parks and streets were full of trees and adorned with flowers and statues. But after the revolution everything changed. Maintenance was abandoned and anything that offered beauty, elegance and luxury, was left to dilapidate. The country was being driven backwards.

My father was relocated to Tripoli, the Libyan Capital. There, we moved into a large detached bungalow within a large plot in an exclusive area called Green Hill. Very quickly, we got to know our neighbours, who were mostly expatriates from Egypt, Germany, Britain, Italy and, of course, Libyans. I remember, soon after, it was decided that all Italian residents were forced to leave the country within 48 hours. They could not take any of their assets, including furniture, and would have no time to deal with their property. Some Italian neighbours of ours decided to sell what furniture they could, as cheaply as possible, to get something to minimise their losses. People were walking in the streets, carrying dining tables, sofas, and armchairs from the Italians' houses to their own. It was chaotic and so very unfair.

I, along with my siblings, was enrolled at the exclusive Tripoli College private school. I enjoyed it and took part in many activities.

One day I was tasked with cutting a large branch, growing from the side of a tree, and given an axe by which to do so. I had thick boots on and a pair of gloves to grip the axe well. Raising the axe, I would bring it down on the branch, repeating the process several times until it was cut off. Four chops later, I looked down at my foot and saw blood squirting out, like a fountain, from an opening in its skin. I had missed the branch and the axe cut through the leather and my skin. Once I saw it, the pain started.

One of the members of staff arrived and decided to call my father. This was not the first time that he had been called to one of my schools to deal with an issue related to me. The last time was in Lexington, where I had pushed a piece of polystyrene into my ear and could not get it out. This time, he had to take me to a hospital where, having satisfied them that the axe missed a major artery, I received three stitches.

There were several expatriate residents, like us, from different countries. Many of their children were of similar ages as we were and befriended us. We attended many parties at their houses and held similar ones at ours. There was always loud music, alcoholic drinks, and some of them had learned that some plant-based items could be used as hallucinogens. They dried banana peels and smoked them as drugs. I must admit, I was persuaded to try them, without feeling any effects.

One of our neighbours was an Egyptian who had just lost his wife and was left with three children to look after on his own. One of his daughters was about a year or two younger than me. She had an older sister and a younger brother. We became friends, spent a lot of times together, and became emotionally close. Semita, my older brother, was also attracted to her sister. Their father worked late, and they used to stay with us during some evenings and we would talk, listen to music, and enjoy each other's company. We were teenagers and our emotions and desires were all over the place. Occasionally, we wanted to be closer physically. I proposed that we treat our gathering as a party with dancing. My mother felt responsible for the girls, but agreed, with the proviso that she would sit with us, albeit while knitting. Although we spent many months developing our feelings, we respected the expected, at least, semi-platonic status.

My parents did not like what was happening in Libya and decided not to stay. They considered going back to the United States, but discovered that we would have to go back to our country of origin before being able to apply for the required visa. As they did not want to do this, an alternative had to be found. My father had heard that the UK was desperate for qualified doctors and valued qualifications. He would have to pass equivalence exams to confirm his ability to practice medicine and to prove that his knowledge was of the same standard as the English ones. After mornings and nights of discussions in bed, my parents decided to move there, where he would also gain higher professional diplomas.

I read several books about England and was not happy with their decision. From these readings and pictures, the country seemed dull with much rain and fog. The houses looked small, with narrow streets, leaving me with the impression of an unfriendly and solitary environment. However, on the 28th of September 1970, we landed at Heathrow Airport in London and found ourselves in a small hotel in Clapham Junction.

Semita and I shared a room. It was around nine o'clock in the evening and my parents, Snats, and Sirkaak were in their rooms. We could not resist going out and exploring Piccadilly Circus, Leicester Square, and Soho, which were highly recommended by the concierge. I asked how we could get there, managed to buy tickets for the underground and travelled to our destinations. It was, probably, the most exciting adventure I had ever had. The first time on a tube, the bright lights of Piccadilly Circus and the hustle and bustle of the big city was beyond compare. Before we realised it, it was eleven o'clock and we had to leave, or the underground would shut. On arrival at the hotel, my mother was there, waiting for us. She was so worried about us being out in a city we knew nothing about so late at night that she slapped me. We were sent to our room, leaving me wondering why it was me whom she smacked and not Semita. Maybe she knew that I, as always, would have been the instigator of the excursion.

We moved into an apartment at Cumberland Court in Marble Arch, in the heart of the city, with Oxford Street, Hyde Park and all the famous sites a few steps away. England proved to be much better than I had expected. Three months later, we moved further afield, taking up residence in a house in Queensbury, a suburb north of London. My father had no job and spent all his time studying and taking exams. I remember having to wake up early in the morning, when it was still dark outside, to help him with his suitcase to the station. He passed his exam of medical equivalence to the British Medical Associations qualifications and proceeded to prepare for the MRCPsych (Member of the Royal College of Psychiatry) requirements.

I was enrolled in a local secondary school, which was made up of two separate buildings, one for boys and the other for girls. Between the two schools was a steel fence, to keep us apart. Like most other boys, joining a couple of friends, I would gravitate towards the fence to chat up the girls on the other side. I had an American accent, which, I guess, made me different, and perhaps intriguing, to others.

One day, a girl invited me to meet her later on in the evening, at a predefined green park in the area. She was with a group of her friends, and they were all laughing. That evening, I left home to go and meet her at the time agreed. It was dark when I got there, with not a soul in sight. In the cold, I waited for over 20 minutes and almost decided to go home, when I noticed a girl walking towards me. She notified me that her friend had never intended to meet me as agreed. She had felt sorry for me and decided to let me know. I thanked her and, disappointed and feeling ridiculed, left. Back home I asked myself why she would have done this. I never asked, nor insisted that we meet. Perhaps this was the English sense of humour? I decided to avoid her and never venture near their school ever again.

My father secured a post in the second-largest city in England, Birmingham. It meant that, yet again, it was all change. Initially, we lived in a house within the hospital grounds where he worked. It was a semi-detached property with a front and back garden and a drive with a garage. Surrounding the buildings was a very large park with the hospital buildings around its perimeter. There was greenery and trees all around us. The house, though smaller than we had become used to, was well decorated, warm, and comfortable. Beyond the front gate, there was a service road and a door in the perimeter wall, leading to Lodge Road. Winson Green, the area in which we lived, was one of the least reputable neighbourhoods due to the prison, which was just a mile east of us.

My father had asked about schools and subsequently sent Semita and me to Harborne Hill Secondary Modern. He had not been told that there were two types of school, Secondary and Grammar, and understood only that, at our ages, we should be in a 'Secondary' school. A couple of months after I joined the school, I realised that the academic subjects I was given were well below my ability. The qualification for which I was working towards was called CSE (Certificate in Secondary Education). It was a lower level to the qualifications, GCE (General Certificate in Education), available at a Grammar school. I chose and was given English, Mathematics, Physics, Chemistry, Woodwork and Metalwork. The choices were limited, dependent on the school timetables.

Very quickly, it became apparent to the teachers that I would excel at everything. However, in my need to belong, I consciously did not strive to do well. Within a few months, I was, barely, above the average there. I managed to get a grade one in Mathematics. However, I only achieved grades two in all the other subjects. This meant that, should I wanted to attend a university, I had to achieve at least four more subjects; at GCE O-Levels.

Unbelievably, yet again, I was forced to move, to the neighbouring town of Wolverhampton, where, along with my sister, I was enrolled into the Wolverhampton Grammar School. There, I was to prepare for my GCE's. I had lost a year and had much work to do to gain the appropriate qualifications to reach what my parents wanted, university. The school was more intellectually challenging than Harborne. However, being new, I spent most of the time making friends and concentrating on social activities.

Three months before I was due to take the final exams, I was called into the headmaster's office. On arrival, I found that he had asked a careers advisor to join us. They asked me what I had planned to do concerning my future; to which I explained that I hope to get my GCE's and continue, after A-Levels, onto university. To my horror, the headmaster informed me that, according to my recent mock exams, it was extremely unlikely that I should pass a single GCE O-Level. The careers advisor asked if I had considered going to the local college to undertake a study in some kind of trade. He went on to explain that there were things like building, plumbing, carpentry, or even electrical installations. I protested and insisted that I would pass my O-Levels this year, study and pass my A-Levels and go on to university. After about half an hour, the meeting was concluded by the headmaster, who said that a letter would be sent to my parents, advising them of the course of action they recommended.

I was more determined than ever to rise to the challenge and prove them wrong. At home, I devised a timetable, which detailed my actions for the following three months to the end of the exams. In it, I planned when I would revise all the necessary topics making up the subjects and included breaks and allowances for any contingencies. I would go to bed at nine p.m. and wake up at five in the morning, following the schedule. I acquired and looked at past exam papers to understand the questions asked and how they were worded. The topics included in the last couple of years' papers were noted and compared to all the topics in all the subjects I was taking. From this analysis, I was able to pick the ones that would most probably be tested in the forthcoming exams. These were the topics I concentrated on studying and included a couple of contingency ones.

I went on to pass the required subjects, followed by the acquisition of four A-Levels, an honours degree (B Eng.), Master's Degree (MBA) and, later on in life, a Postgraduate Certificate in Education (PGCE). Where would I be now, had I accepted my Headmaster's assessment of my abilities and followed his recommendations?

My parents had always insisted that I studied Medicine or Engineering at University. I chose Engineering, as I did not want to follow in my father's footsteps, and was accepted by Sheffield University to study my choice of subject, which was Electronics. At the time, the government paid all tuition fees and offered students a maintenance grant, the value of which was determined by the parents' wealth and status. In my case, I was to get the minimum and my father had to top it up to the recommended amount. He questioned the Government's recommended amount, informing me that he would give me only half of it.

It was summer and I was temporarily working in the warehouse for a company called Salisbury Handbags Limited. Apart from unloading and storing boxes of goods, I joined the drivers, helping to deliver the products to the various shops around London. I had worked for them, during the holidays, for over three years, and became well known to everyone.

When my father told me about the 'pittance' he was going to give me to live on, I felt that, perhaps, I should not go to university. I had visions of not enjoying the experience that came with the study, and would always feel disadvantaged, not being able to enjoy the life that, well off students, enjoyed, nor that of those who were given the full grant. I felt bitter towards my father for putting me into this situation.

I mentioned this to the manager of the Marble Arch branch of the company in which I worked, and to my surprise, he offered me the position of Assistant Manager. I would get, what appeared to be a good wage that would render me independent, not needing a handout from my parents. I had a lot of thinking to do, as this would be a life-changing move. Before the final decision, I felt that I had to discuss it with my father.

When I mentioned it to him, he appeared to be shocked. As always, he had expected me to do as I was told, and to accept whatever he decided to give me, without question. He obviously wanted me to go to university and feared that I was making a mistake by considering anything else. After a short period of discussions, he asked me to prepare a budget, showing my likely expenditure whilst at university; following this, we would resume our talk and decide what to do. The following day, we sat down with the budget, and he scrutinised it. It was almost the same amount recommended by the Government. After some further debate, he agreed to give me, what was 75% of the recommended amount.

The decision was mine, and was the most difficult one I had had to take at that time. I got a piece of paper and drew up two columns split down the middle, titled 'university' and 'work.' I proceeded to write down the pros and cons of each choice. In the end, university won, as it would result in better long-term benefits. Although I would have to work during the holidays to make up 'drinking and entertainment' money, I would have a wider choice of employment, gain more knowledge and exposure and, eventually, better financial independence. It was the best decision I had ever made.

Following graduation with a second-class honours degree – in those days this was deemed to be very good, as only half of those who joined the degree course completed it, only a couple of students got a first class honours, and a few second. I declined to continue, as suggested by my Tutor, to a master's degree, but wanted to stay in Yorkshire, where I had spent the last four years, and came to call it my hometown.

Whilst at Sheffield University, I was invited to one of the parties held by my friends. There, a girl who asked if I knew someone called Jenny approached me. She was tall and slim, with long blonde hair and blue eyes, and, reminded me of a large doll my sister had with the same-coloured eyes and hairstyle. Apparently, she was supposed to meet her, but could not find her. We talked, drank, and danced, excluding everybody else, all night. Our friendship blossomed into affection and, after the first year, we decided to move in together. I left my lovely hall of residence, with all its comforts and surrounding greenery and pond, to a ground floor flat in an old Victorian terraced house, a short distance away from the campus. Studying music, she graduated a year before me and started to study for a Post Graduate teaching certificate. We decided to get married immediately after my graduation.

Her mother was a strong woman, not working, but definitely the influencer and leader of the household. Although both parents showed friendliness and affection for me as their daughter's boyfriend, they cleverly hid their true feelings. There were several disagreements and upsets leading up to the wedding. They were, as we were, middle class, with the father working as an IT manager at a large, well-known British company. The wedding ceremony reflected this status, with 85% of the guests from her side of the family and friends, whereas only my parents, brothers, sister, and a couple of my very close friends attended. Her father's speech lasted about 30 minutes, mostly talking about my parents and father's position and accomplishments. Very quickly after the meal, my wife and I were ordered by her mother to leave for the airport as it would not be good to keep everyone at the venue for too long. We had to wait four hours before we could board our flight at the scheduled time.

That day was the first time that both parents had met and, apart from a few moments throughout the celebrations, they had not really managed to get to know each other that well. After we got back from honeymoon, my mother told me that, shortly after we left, Janna's parents had asked a few close friends to go to their house for a gathering with some nibbles. They asked my parents, but my mum felt, their invitation was not sincere and that they had to alert them that they did not know where they lived. They described roughly where they were going and assured them that they would lead them there. However, they drove so quickly that my parents almost got lost; apparently that was their intention. When they got to their house, there was only one armchair left vacant. Mum sat down and, seeing my father without a seat, asked him to sit on the arm of her chair. Janna's mum went running to them shouting at him for sitting there as he might break the chair. After a few, very difficult, embarrassing, solitary minutes, my parents decided to leave, never to see them again.

Two years later, feeling life together had become unsustainable, I told Janna that we should leave each other. Her parents were staying with us that night and heard us arguing and shouting. The following morning, her mother asked me if I slept well, to which I replied that, considering her daughter and I deciding to leave each other, no. To my surprise, her reply was a cool, "Well, let's see how we can make this as easy as possible…" After some time, it became obvious that she never wanted her daughter to marry me and that she preferred her son-in-law to be a "white, blue-eyed Englishman." This was a realisation that reinforced itself several times throughout my adult working career.

Work, Challenges and Prejudices

Whilst at University, I had carried out industrial training at Philips Electronics as a trainee Radio Production Testing Engineer. I was supervised by a very enthusiastic, knowledgeable, and caring head of department, who not only taught me well, but was also the reason for my liking and wanting to work for Philips when I graduate. Fortunately, when I was looking for a job meeting my criteria of staying in Yorkshire, Philips offered me the position of a Work Study Engineer in one of their subsidiaries, Philips Domestic Appliances, in Hipperholm, West Yorkshire.

Like all international conglomerates in those days, Philips believed very much in excellent training. As soon as I started, I was sent on an induction event at their headquarters in London. Two days were spent getting to know all there is about the company, its vision, financial standing, products, divisions, and personnel. Back at Philips Domestic Appliances, specialist programme, again learning all about their products of washing machines and tumble driers – how they worked and were manufactured and packaged. I was also enrolled on a professional course, leading to a Work Study Practitioner's diploma. Initially concentrating on production, I was able to transform the manufacturing process. Instead of a single, continuous, 'production line,' I created several modules in which machines were completely assembled. Each module comprised five operators, trained to build a whole machine from scratch. One of the operators would wheel a trolley around a common central bay, called the supermarket, collecting all the large parts required for assembly of a machine. He/she would return to the first location within the module. Using the necessary components, made available to each location, as needed, the main body of the machine is assembled. That partly assembled machine is passed on to the operators within the module, to assemble their allocated parts, until the finished machine was complete and transferred to packaging and eventually, distribution. This method increased productivity by at least 25%, improving yield and profitability. Each group within the module, felt in competition with the others. A major part of this project was the designing of fixtures and fittings to aid in manufacturing and improved efficiency, and complete training of the operators.

In order to assess productivity and maximise resource allocation and uses, a 'standard time' for each task must be derived. This was achieved by selecting an experienced operator, breaking down his, or her job into smaller tasks, and timing how long it took to complete each one. Ultimately, the time taken to assemble a machine was derived. Attention was paid to the method used and other factors that might complicate the operation in order to derive the 'standard time' needed to complete any or all parts of the assembly. The information is used to establish an accurate cost of manufacture, a comparison tool to aid in method improvements and information enabling management to offer incentives to the workforce, encouraging them to produce more.

Computerisation was very young in those days. I embraced the introduction of the first PC to be used in the division. Through appropriate programming, I was able to carry out various analytical tasks and produce management reporting to monitor performance and further improve production. This had never happened at Philips Domestic Appliances and helped the division stand out for their management information and reporting excellence.

I had three colleagues in the department, who helped me with my initial training and became really good friends. Each person was given a production department for which he was responsible. However, my technological skills and ability to understand and complete any tasks necessary quickly resulted in me being given more responsibility, transcending all the departments.

However, I was given no promotion, or salary increases to reflect the achievements. After several disappointments, I just could not understand why.

The company had a social club for use by staff during non-working hours. It was very active, holding several events, including Christmas and other dinners, outings, and competitions, like it's a 'knockout', swimming, and other sporting ones. All this contributed to a superb feeling of comradeship and belonging, leading to a sense of loyalty and a more productive workforce.

Being very sociable and really interested in people, I talked to everyone – both on the shop floor and within the offices. My foreign background, accent, and ability to listen helped me become well known. Activities arranged by the social club were always attended, particularly sporting competitions. My past swimming expertise helped me to win a company-wide competition.

As a new graduate, I was very ambitious. Due to our numerous moves around the country and internationally, I was three years behind where I should be. When I discussed this with my manager, he informed me that there would be no way that I could be promoted. Furthermore, it would be impossible to become a manager before the age of 30. I was only 25 and could not see much progression over the next five years. I had been given great annual reviews, felt that I had contributed more than my job required and was ready and able for promotion and a more challenging position. In meetings, I would make recommendations that were ignored, only for someone else's suggestions, exactly as the ones I voiced, worded slightly differently, being enthusiastically accepted. I was made to feel that, no matter how much I achieved and can offer to the company, I would not be appropriately rewarded. This led me, in desperation, to start looking out for opportunities, which may not necessarily be within Philips, or Yorkshire.

Very quickly, a company was advertising for a Group Industrial Engineer in Hampshire. The salary was 40% more than what I was earning, plus a fully expensed company car. Meatpack Hampshire Group belonged to a large frozen food conglomerate called BEEGAM. The opportunity seemed too good to ignore. Working for a newly created department, I would be responsible for maximising company resources spread over three divisions. The south of England was an attractive place, warmer, sunnier and near the sea. Three interviews later, I was offered the position and accepted it.

We sold our modern terraced house in Wakefield and bought a link-detached house in an estate in Fair Oak, near Eastleigh. The head office in which I was based was within one of the factories in Chandler's Ford. Its main activity was to package frozen meat, including beef, lamb, pork, and chicken, in the three branches spread over the southern part of England. My commute from home was only a 20-minute drive and I reported to who I believed was the best manager I ever had. I was very happy in this job and felt a liking and respect from all employees, senior, or otherwise.

Production processes, including machinery and productivity, were identified as requiring urgent attention. I decided to quantify the time required to complete each job, with the best and most efficient methods of doing so. Having done this, output was increased, costs reduced and, thus, profitability increased. The workers had not been too rushed to complete their tasks. By carrying out the studies performed at Philips, I was able to quantify the length of time each task should take and how much work each operator can complete in an hour. The production manager and I worked together to create new methods of carrying out the necessary operations. I drew a new production floor layout and identified machinery to speed packaging, reduce waste and improve quality.

We knew it would be difficult to expect everyone to work to the new, higher set standards. So, we started with intensive training, followed by the announcement of an incentive scheme, which rewarded those who would perform to the highest levels, in terms of quality and efficiency.

Later, the focus changed, concentrating on the use of machinery and advances in production to further increase capacity.

From discussions with personnel, and observations, one important vacuum packaging machine had never worked at more than 50% of its capacity. It caused a great deal of downtime and lost opportunities for sales. I asked to meet with the Engineering Maintenance Manager and asked him to observe the machine in operation with me. As expected, there were several issues and it kept stopping.

I said, "This must be frustrating for you, as I know it is for the operators and me." I had to be careful that he did not think that I was directly criticising him. So, I added how he had done a great job in installing the new machinery and keeping production going through the renovation and development period. "Do you think you could get this, reasonably old, but very loyal, machine to consistently deliver a minimum efficiency of say, at least 85%?" I questioned. He said that he was sure he could and called his assistants, ordering them to work on nothing else but this until they made it work effectively. Within three days, the machine started working well. Rarely, after the overhaul, did this much-used piece of equipment fail.

Very soon afterwards, I was called into the general manager's office, and, to my surprise, he asked me if I would take charge of an ailing production department. I was thrilled by his confidence in me and accepted the Production Manager's role. This reminded me of my boss at Philips informing me that there was no way of this happening before the age of 30. Now, at 27, I had achieved management status. Indeed, a few years later, throughout industry, there were many 'Managers' aged well below 30.

My new position reported to a newly appointed plant manager, with whom, unfortunately, I did not get on. He had just joined the company and, from previous encounters, I had no confidence in his abilities. My previous industrial engineering manager was excellent, knowing exactly how to deal with people, was supportive, motivating, honest, fair and knew his job extremely well. Thankfully, my feelings about the new manager were shared by some of my colleagues, so it was not just a subordinate's point of view. On our daily walks around the department, he would speak in what I felt was a derogatory way to some operators. When I tried to explain what he meant with more sensitivity, I would be chastised for being too harsh. I could not understand this.

The General Manager and his senior team decided to buy out the business from BEEGAM. In fear of working for a new, riskier organisation and, more importantly, dislike of my new manager, I embarked on a search for a new job. I decided to return to a large multinational, where there would be more training and better prospects. They would also be much less likely to fail, providing more security. I was offered the role of industrial engineer at Gillette Europe's head office in Isleworth, West London. Apart from the advantages and reputation such a company offered, I would not have to work under that horrible manager again.

When I resigned, the General Manager asked to see me. He had not known of my unhappiness and desire to leave but now wanted me to reconsider. In the discussion which followed, he applauded my achievements to date and said that I had "excellent potential within the company." He informed me that I was the only person who was liked and respected, receiving only praise by everyone in the company. He continued, suggesting that perhaps I would consider becoming the head of what would be a newly created Human Resources Department. Sadly, and despite being very grateful for his confidence in me, I did not accept and left. Having kept in contact with most colleagues there, I heard that the manager I disliked was sacked very soon after I left.

Gillette was much larger, with a multi-level hierarchal structure and many more separate departments. My first brief was to reorganise the whole of the production facilities and stores. It was a mammoth task, which necessitated the relocation of several huge, multi-tonne machines and adding four large packaging machines. I spent the first three months learning all about razor blade making, and became familiar with every single process required for their production, quality control, packaging, storage and despatch. It was a huge project unlike any I have ever been part of. Support from my manager was minimal, and so I had to determine the personnel who could help and approach them.

My first task was to set a plan of the work, timing, and process necessary to ensure success. Armed with this, I met with the Manufacturing Manager to explain my plan and gained his support, placing various personnel under my leadership. They included specialists in all the activities that were necessary to complete the whole project.

Interaction between all departments within the building was vital. Apart from the obvious manufacturing section, Marketing, Purchasing, and Finance were very frequent contacts. The following three months were spent measuring and drawing every single floor space, machinery, heights, entrances and exits to facilitate the new layout and packaging facilities. The new packaging machines' specifications were also acquired and used. Six months later, the new production department was completely reorganised. One section I had designed within the production floor was an elevated, decorated staff canteen equipped with modern tables and chairs. The inclusion of plants led to the employees describing it as 'Samasem's Oasis,' in honour of my origin and their belief that I had lived in the desert. A great many of the employees thought that, in Egypt, I lived in a tent and that camels were our form of transport.

The project was a huge success, finishing on time and below budget. It also resulted in cost savings, due to the newly designed layout, requiring fewer operators. Sadly, despite having proved myself in this, and continuing to do so with other tasks and projects given, my boss decided to employ a Senior Industrial Engineer from outside the organisation. Five years after graduation, with experience at Philips, proof of success and abilities at Meatpack, and now over a year at Gillette, I was not considered for promotion. Devastated, I was left wondering what it was that I needed to do or, what did I do wrong? The person who was employed to the senior position had finished his education with a diploma in engineering and had no supervisory experience. I started to wonder if it had anything to do with me being the only non-English person within Manufacturing and Engineering? Little did I know that this was actually the case all over the company!

My thoughts and self-search led me to the belief that I needed to gain a higher qualification; something that would arm me with the best knowledge about Businesses and tools necessary for their success. My ambition was to reach the highest position in a company. Following some research, I decided that an MBA (Master's degree in Business Administration) would be the best, most highly sought after and respected acquisition. It teaches one all about business policies, tools, and success; it is also valued by the best organisations. People with this qualification attract the best, most challenging jobs and remunerations.

Following a search for educational establishments that offer this course for people at work, I found a limited few. The first one I chose required attendance at university on one afternoon during the week and some weekends and would last for eighteen months. Knowing this, I arranged to meet my manager to ask him to allow me to take the afternoon off to complete the course, offering to work over every other day of the week to make up any lost time. Sadly, he was not sympathetic. He told me that he had no qualifications and, why, then, did I feel that I needed even more qualifications than I had. He denied my request for the reason that he did not have or need a degree, and it would not benefit his department. But if, as I suspected then, he was intimidated by my qualifications, why did he hire me? Did he decide, after my apparent success, that he had made a mistake, leading him to the decision to employ the senior person, instead of promoting me? Or was it some other prejudice?

I had three options. The first was to give up on the idea and continue to work hard in the hope that I would eventually get promoted. The second was to look for another job, and the third, to find another institution that would offer me the course without having to take time off work. I chose the latter and after further searches, I found Middlesex Business School. The course was three evenings a week, plus some weekends. I would be able to complete the qualifications in three years. This was to turn out to be the most difficult three years in my early career.

Along with some of my fellow students, I had to work hard all day and attend Middlesex for three evenings every week and give up two weekends every month. There were also the numerous assignments, requiring study and research to complete, leaving very little time to carry out any household chores, never mind social or family activities. There was a constant feeling of guilt when I did not study and felt equally bad for not spending leisure time with my partner, friends, and family. There were exams, assignments, and a final project. Every year I would seriously consider giving it up. However, when I thought about my goals, the way I had been treated at work and the key such a qualification would offer me in opening the right doors, I decide to continue in the pursuit of a better future and carry on.

During the final year, on my way home in Ealing, my motorbike skidded out of control, crashing to the ground, leaving me with a badly broken leg. After about three weeks of total agony, I felt well enough to hold meetings with my colleagues to enable a project to be completed. The benefits of this project to the company were huge. However, they could not find anyone else to take it over and successfully complete it. Six weeks later, with a cast covering my whole leg, up to my thigh, using crutches, I decided to take taxis to go to work. Sadly, I also developed a cataract in both eyes and was waiting for an operation to treat the most affected one. To complete my final exam, a desk had to be set up for me at the back of the exam hall, with an extra chair to support my plastered leg and an extra lamp, producing bright light, to help me read and write. Despite all these mishaps and work pressures, I was able to successfully complete my MBA.

I had specialised in Marketing, as it was this profession that excited me and in which I felt I would be successful. A good part of the MBA was biased towards finance, and, in the course of my work, I had made friends with a senior member of the finance department who saw potential in me and felt that I would be capable of working with them. Following my qualifications, they had a vacancy and offered me the post of Financial Analyst in the Northern European division at a salary that was 30% higher than that which I had been given. How could I refuse? Hard work and persistence really do pay off.

It is worth mentioning here that, after my move from the Engineering department, Gillette issued a prerequisite of a bachelor's degree qualification for any employee in a similar position to my earlier Industrial Engineering one or higher. This meant that neither my old boss nor the newly employed Senior Engineer would be promoted further. Their replacements would have to satisfy the required degree qualification. Neither the company nor I felt that people without higher qualifications were less able than those who have them. Rather, competition for jobs and the huge number of applicants forced organisations to find a way to reduce shortlisting easily and quickly. Only about ten out of two hundred applicants would have the higher qualifications. This was much easier to handle for recruiters. The benefit to the company is better knowledge and more determined candidates, who will achieve more.

I worked hard to prove myself in this new field, and within six months I was promoted to the European Division. Two years later, I spoke to my supervisor, Predepe, about needing more challenge and responsibility. He told me that he had been in this field for five years before he became a supervisor. Five years later, and he continues to be in the same position. My knowledge of him and observations highlighted that he was British born, of Indian origin, and that all middle and senior managers were white Britons, Western Europeans, or Americans. Again, it became apparent that further opportunities for promotions for me, were limited. I managed to utilise the marketing specialisation gained from the MBA by working closely with that department within Gillette Europe. I manoeuvred my tasks to become involved with a very important project, with the objective of finding a system that would price the products taking account of the differing currencies within the continent. I learned a great deal about how currency is used to purchase a product in one country, at a certain exchange rate, only to gain an advantage of another country's weaker rate. Before the Euro, it was a nightmare to control cross-country pricing. The project was a success, and I approached the head of the department to ask if I could work with him. To my surprise, I was informed that, at 33, I was too old to start. Also, I realised that all members of that department were native English or European expatriates. Again, I am left with the feeling of discrimination, which haunted me through-out the years in which I lived in England. Although I was liked, or, perhaps, tolerated, I never really felt that I belonged. Most of my so-called friends would spend a very good evening in the Pub, and the following morning would show a disregard, or un-friendliness, that reinforced the feeling of not being included. I had to be twenty times better than anyone to be respected and given an opportunity.

I had to remain in my role but kept thinking that I had worked hard and gained valuable technical, commercial, and supervisory experience, and what was arguably the most sought-after busi-ness qualification. My English was fluent, with perhaps a slight accent, and I was of a reasonably fair complexion. So, why could I not see a clear path to more senior and challenging positions? I was confident that I could do this; but how? Perhaps, if I wait-ed another five years, I may be able to secure a position, as an expatriate, in one of Gillette's international divisions, or some-thing might change, enabling me to become a supervisor in the finance department.

Although, I had lived in Egypt only in my childhood days, I could speak Arabic fluently. So, when the General Manager of the Egyptian Division of Gillette visited us in the UK, I met him, expressing an interest in joining the marketing department there, or any other options. After half an hour of questioning by him, mainly about my personal background, including religion, he did not refuse. However, he informed me that he would only be able to offer me a local salary, which would equate to £2000 per year and was considered to be high relative to salaries in that country. I was earning about £18,000, with a mortgage, requiring £4,500 per annum to service. He would not offer me an expatri-ate position, which would have meant an annual remuneration, for anyone nominated from within Gillette Europe, of approximately £25000, tax-free, plus accommodation, company car and driver and annual return flights to the UK.

Very disappointed and feeling that the doors to better positions within Gillette were closed and bolted, I did not know what to do next. Even the best key there was, gained via the MBA, would not be able to unlock any of them. Then, suddenly, I saw an advert in the Telegraph newspaper for a Business and Operations Development Manager, for the Middle East, Africa, and Indian sub-continent regions. Reporting to the region's General Manager of a multi-national American Conglomerate, the description of the person and experiences only lacked my name. The job and person specifications matched every qualification, knowledge and experience I had. One important requirement was the ability to speak Arabic, as well as English, fluently. It was the ideal job, I could not resist.

I was invited to a first interview, followed by a second one. The questions asked were very trying and the more I answered the more difficult they became. Every answer was documented, appearing to show a well-planned, organised and executed employment process to attract, as was specified, the best candidate. I really wanted the job and what it offered in terms of not only remuneration but, more importantly, challenge, variety, and potential. To my delight, I was offered the post and informed that I had beaten 120 other hopefuls. The joy and feeling of confidence flowed through me like never before.

When I handed in my resignation from Gillette, I was surprised at their reaction. They did not want me to go and offered me an extra 15% increase on my salary. They had been very happy with my performance and felt that most of my colleagues within Europe liked me and respected my analysis and reporting. Unfortunately, it was too late. I had decided that the new job would suit me much, much more. I would use all my knowledge, qualifications, and business and linguistic skills in what appeared to be a wonderful job. Also, the challenges and exposure of such a role would equip me with valuable tools with which I could achieve more.

The Ideal Job - If Only

Following my one month's notice period I moved to the new company's divisional headquarters at the foot of Windsor Castle. The building was made up of two floors. I would occupy the downstairs office with my boss' office, secretary and conference rooms being upstairs. My manager, Darren, was not available, as he was travelling. The secretary and I were the only ones in the building so, she showed me around, filled me in on the organisation and pointed me to items I may need, related to the new job. I was shown, the interview file where the conclusion was written about me, stating, "…he stood out from all the rest…" The report noted that my answers to the questions, and evident ability, plus potential, impressed my new manager and were well above anyone else's. It felt good and motivating to read this.

During my first two weeks, my boss continued to be out of the country. He had not left any instructions as to what I should do. I had no idea what the work really involved and had to guess as to what information I needed to gather. Apart from the information about the group, the overall company structure and some files related to our division, I had a copy of my job description. Having read it, I started to research my target countries and find out as much as I could about their socio-economic and political ideology. I read about two joint ventures we had in Saudi Arabia, gathering as much information about them, their activities and present status as I could. Finally, my boss returned from his travels, and I was asked to meet him in his office.

During our first meeting, I was given more information about the organisation, its operations and structure. We discussed the division's activities, its existing joint ventures in Saudi and how he saw my responsibilities. Basically, I was to investigate countries in The Middle East, North Africa, India and Bangladesh, with a view of establishing joint ventures with partners within them. Another part of my job was to monitor and support the existing joint ventures, helping them to develop and grow. It all sounded very exciting, and I could hardly wait to start my job. On a personal level, we seemed to gel, conversing with ease and feeling comfortable with our discussions.

He took out a document about company cars and asked me to choose one for quick delivery. In the meantime, the division for providing the cars to the managers would deliver a temporary one for me to use until mine was ready. Finally, he informed me that he would be taking me with him on a trip to Istanbul in Turkey, and Dammam and Jeddah, in Saudi Arabia. The secretary arranged the flights and hotel bookings; all business class and five-star accommodation, commencing in ten days. This was to be my first international business trip, spanning more than one continent! I was very excited and could not wait to get into the work.

During this time, I arranged to visit the Department of Trade and Industry in London, and contacted various organisations specialising in the packaging industry in the target countries. This enabled me to form a better understanding of their performances, compile socio-economic data and tabulate it, to identify my priorities for visiting these countries. My aim was to maximise company benefits, contributing to its development and success, with minimal costs.

Socially, I got to know my boss a little better, and the office's location in the middle of Windsor gave me opportunities for exploring sights during lunchtimes. Most of my work at that stage involved traveling to various companies and offices within the Southeast, establishing contacts and gathering valuable information. It could not be better.

On the day of my departure with Darren, a limousine arrived at my home and transported me to Heathrow Airport, where, after check-in, I met him in the business class lounge. It was wonderful. A very bright, large area compartmented into separated spaces for working, eating, or just lounging on comfortable sofas and chairs. There were newspapers, TVs, and business communication equipment. There was a bar, with all the alcoholic and soft drinks you could want, and a very lavish buffet filled with cold and hot food for everyone to enjoy. It was like being in a five-star hotel. Waiters were available to serve and pamper you. We made full use of the facilities and waited to be called for boarding our flight. Our first stop was Istanbul and a two-night stay. Appointments were made to introduce me to a number of the companies with whom we work, and my boss's contacts. Also, we would visit a couple of beverage-filling plants, including Pepsi Cola, one of our customers.

In Istanbul, we stayed at a luxurious hotel with rooms overlooking the Bosporus. We visited all the contacts and they seemed to welcome me like a new acquaintance. I learned a great deal from the factories and the various people showing me their operations. Later, we had a chance to see some of the sights in Istanbul and had a fantastic fish dinner in a luxurious restaurant overlooking the Bosporus before we had to move on.

We got to the island of Bahrain, from which we had to be driven across a long bridge into Saudi Arabia. However, as it was Saudi's weekend, the offices were closed and staff not available until Sunday. So, we had to stay at the Le Meridian hotel, which overlooked the sea, for two nights. The island lacked greenery, with what was seen all over England replaced with sand. It was very hot, and we spent the days around the pool just talking, eating, and drinking. It was very pleasant, and we seemed to get on very well. Before long, it was Sunday and the driver from Saudi came to pick us up. We had to cross the long bridge connecting Bahrain to Dammam in Saudi Arabia. The whole trip would last just under an hour.

The driver was an Arab and could not speak much English, if any. It had been 27 years since I lived in Saudi and was eager to hear about its development and get to know about how people now lived. As the driver's English was so poor, we spoke in Arabic throughout most of the journey. I was careful to translate everything to my boss so that he did not feel left out, and also benefited from the interesting stories and information offered by the driver. He told me how things were, how long he had worked for the company, whom he had driven, what people normally do in their daily lives in Saudi and many other very interesting tales. I was glad for the talk, as not only did it pass the time and result in more knowledge, I also got to practice my Arabic.

We got to the Offices of our Dammam Saudi venture partners. There, again, I had a very warm, friendly, successful introduction. Quite a lot of Arabic was used when various members of the group spoke to me. Where I thought it was important, I translated some of the comments to my boss. They had prepared a very lavish lunch for us. On the very large dining table, there was an enormous tray filled with special rice surrounding a small, whole cooked lamb – obviously, this had not changed since 1960. There must have been about twenty serving dishes, filled with exotic food, laid out.

After this feast, we were taken to the joint-venture factory, CCSA. It manufactured what are known as two-piece beverage cans, made of aluminium. I was in awe at the size of the machines within the line that manufactured the cans. At one end a large coil of aluminium sheet was fed into a huge 'press'. It cut circular discs which were drawn and wall-ironed, forming the body of the can. They passed through other machines, and were washed, coated with protective lacquers, and printed on the outside with the customers' labels before the necks and flanges were formed so that the lid can be securely seamed on after they were filled. Finally, a machine was used to place them on a pallet and wrap them securely, before moving them into storage for eventual despatch to the customer, such as Pepsi, Coca-Cola, and other beverage companies. Less than 10 people supervised and operated the whole process, which was capable of producing over 2000 cans per minute.

Following the tour and further discussions with the staff, we were driven to the hotel, owned by the Saudi partner. Again, it was a lavish, 5-star accommodation in which we were given extra attention as requested by the owner. It had been a long day and we were due to leave in the morning.

On the following morning, we flew from Dammam to Jeddah. Whilst in Africa, India, or the Middle East, company policy was to travel first class. A superb experience, but it only lasted for one hour. When we got there, a driver met and drove us straight to the second joint venture, JBCMC. After meeting the Senior Management team, I was taken for yet another tour around the factory, which was very similar to the Dammam one, though somewhat more modern. After the tour, I was informed that my boss wanted to see me in the General Manager's office. I walked in to find him sitting behind the desk with no one else in the room. After shutting the door and sitting down, what was said made me feel as if someone had poured a bucket of ice over my head.

He started by saying, "This is not working out, and I am afraid you will have to go." The shock rendered me speechless for a few seconds and I just stared at him. "Perhaps you can go back to Gillette," he went on. After another moment's pause, I replied that of course I could not just go back to Gillette and thought that everything was going well. He replied that it would be difficult for us to work together. I asked why and if there was anything that we could do to fix things. "I do not need to do anything, I am the boss!" he shouted. I could not believe what was happening. Everything apparently went well in Turkey, Bahrain and Saudi, until today. However, it seemed that he had made up his mind that I could not continue working with him. For the remainder of the visit, I was told to spend time with the managers, look around the factory and get to know the operations.

Most of the personnel within the offices were Egyptians, Arabs, Indians, and Filipinos. The Finance Manager was Egyptian and the Sales Manager, Indian. The General Manager, Plant Manager, the most senior ones, and Supervisors, were all British, and the rest of the shop floor workers were mostly Indians or, Filipinos.

A good many of these were highly qualified graduates, with some, possessing Medical Degrees. They could not get work, or enough salary back home. Workers in these, blue-collar jobs were only given single status visas, leaving their families behind. I discussed all aspects of the operations with everyone and found out that there were many issues affecting efficiency and productivity, not to mention staff morale.

On the following day, my boss had to travel for a meeting with someone and I had to travel back home on my own. In the morning, I boarded the plane and retuned to the UK. Back in the office, I was not sure what to expect. Would I stay or be told to go? My boss was not there, leaving only the secretary and I in the building. I reviewed my notes and findings at JBCMC and, over the two days before the weekend, had finished a report with my findings, including a conclusion and recommendations for further action. I had to overcome my feelings of rejection and fear of being thrown out after only two months, without any job to go to. Perhaps, I could return to Gillette and grovel, in the hope that they would take me back; after all, they had not wanted me to leave.

On Monday, my boss returned and, in the afternoon, called me to his office. I could hardly climb the stairs from my pounding heart and my legs, weak and shaking. It felt as if I was walking up to the gallows, to be guillotined. Eventually, I was there, closed the door and sat in front of him. After a long silent pause, I was prepared to hear the worst. Finally, he spoke and for a few seconds, I could not believe what was being said. He informed me that I would be sent to our Head Office in Chicago, USA. There I would learn everything about the company and its products and be trained in the process and manufacture of two-piece beverage cans.

"Is this guy schizophrenic?" I thought. At the same time, I felt as if an enormous weight had been lifted off my shoulders and saw a glimmer of hope. Unfortunately, he would not elaborate further, informing me that he had to leave and would be away for the rest of the week. I was booked to travel on Sunday and expected to continue with whatever it was I was doing until then.

On the day of travel, a driver in a limousine collected me and drove to the airport. Meanwhile, I decided to forget the dark cloud which had been hanging over me for the last three weeks. Booked on the Virgin Atlantic flight to Chicago, with a seat in 'Upper class," at check-in I was given an invitation to visit the 'Business Class' lounge, and stayed until I was called for boarding. Whilst there, I enjoyed several drinks, together with a selection of hot and cold food. Boarding was announced and I, along with the other passengers from the lounge, headed to the gate. Virgin Atlantic was fairly new and, to everyone's surprise, Richard Branson was there, in person, greeting the passengers. I had heard and read about him and, at that moment, he surpassed all description and proved his worth. He greeted me and wished me an enjoyable trip, asking that, should I need anything, or have any issues, to report it to the head stewardess. The seats were more like luxurious armchairs, offering plenty of space around them. I was led to my chosen window seat and served a glass of champagne. There were toiletries bags for each passenger, filled with a razor, toothpaste and brush, aftershave, soap, and a comb. After take-off, we were invited to the upper deck of this Boeing 747 plane, where there was a bar, fully stocked with all the alcoholic and non-alcoholic beverages one can imagine. There was a round table with hors d'oeuvres surrounded by very comfortable armchairs. It was like being in the lounge of a luxury hotel in the air.

When I eventually arrived in Chicago, completed immigration, collected my bag, and headed outside the airport, I saw a guy who was holding a sign with my name on it. I approached him, identifying myself, had my bag taken from me and was led to a car, which was to take me to my hotel. It was very near Lake Michigan in a very central location, encouraging me to spend the day, resting and exploring the area. Whilst having breakfast, on the following morning, I received a message informing me that a driver would pick me up at 9:30.

The driver was very punctual, and it took us about 20 minutes to get to the company. The very pleasant Human Resources

Manager met me with a warm greeting. He took me for a tour around the building, introducing me to various personnel, before heading back to his office. There, I was shown a presentation about the company, its origins, products, personnel, international divisions and its vision and future strategy. A couple of hours later, following a fairly in-depth conversation about my background, I was taken to another building and introduced to some of the senior managers, spending about ten minutes with each. They told me more about the company and their objectives and asked me about my views, trip, and the Windsor office. The Plant Manager arrived and accompanied us to lunch. We had a great time, eating good, well-prepared food and chatting about England, the US and company, amongst many other things. It felt completely different from my latest discussions with my boss in Saudi and Windsor.

The next three weeks were spent in the factory with various people, learning all about the manufacture and technical aspects of what is called a two-piece can – the body and the top or lid. I was, also, taken to other manufacturing sites producing some of the other products manufactured by the parent company, CCC. These included the manufacture and composition of beverage paper cups and plastic containers, used mainly by the Oil companies.

Over the following three weeks, I was given folders containing company policies and procedures to read. This was supplemented by extensive on the job training in the steps of beverage can production and technical details. During the final week, it seemed as if I was being tested on how well I had understood the commercial as well as the technical aspects of the operations.

I must admit, it wasn't all work, 24 hours a day. I toured Chicago and experienced its well-known strong, cold winds. There were several parks, together with the lake, which were a treasure to walk through, enjoy the scenery, or just soak in the atmosphere. On occasion, it was so cold the fountains froze, forming artistic formations. One evening I booked to watch the Nutcracker Suite ballet and was mesmerised. On another weekend day, I drove the car to the state of Kentucky. There, I travelled into Lexington, where I managed to visit North Arcadia Park, where I saw the house we lived in and reminisced about the old days and my adventures there. The house and block were the same. However, 30 years on, most people we knew had gone, although none of us would have remembered each other. Still, it was good to see the town, in which I saw some of my happiest days.

I never felt lonely or bored. During my stay, I was invited to dinner, either at a restaurant, or house of one of the managers at least twice or three times a week. The HR Manager invited me to his home, where I was introduced to and ate dinner with his wife and children. This was followed by a retreat to one of their living rooms, where we drank wine and beer and chatted about everything. It was very enjoyable. On another evening, I was invited to a restaurant with the Plant Manager and his wife. The following week, it was the Vice President's turn. He invited me to a very exclusive restaurant. Together with his wife, we spent at least two hours eating drinking and talking about them, Chicago, international travels and, in more depth, me and my work and personal experiences and achievements. During the final week, more gatherings with the HR Manager and his wife and other managers took place. On my final day at the plant, there was a small gathering to wish me bon voyage. I felt as if I was part of a family and wished I could have lived and worked there, instead of in England. The HR Manager drove me to the airport for the flight home. He was extremely friendly and genuine.

I returned to England and the quiet Windsor office. Again, Darren was not around so I told the secretary about my trip. In my office I read through my notes and sent correspondences to everyone in Chicago, thanking them for the fantastic hospitality they had offered me during my visit. I could not, however, stop thinking about when or if my boss would ask me to leave. I loved what my new job entailed, the people I met on my travels and the company itself and I could not imagine going back to Gillette and groveling. These thoughts had always been with me, but I had to push them back in order to act naturally whilst with others.

On his return, Darren called me back to his office. The same thoughts filled my head and I had to consciously relax and try to be positive. As usual, with a straight face and serious look, my boss asked me to come in, close the door and sit down. As I did, he appeared to be slightly at ease and more friendly. He asked me about how my trip went, to which I replied that it was very good and informative. Following further discussion, lasting about half an hour, he started to say that, perhaps, we could start over again and continue as normal. It was lunchtime and he asked me if I would like to join him for a pub lunch. I could not believe what I was hearing and, with absolute joy and delight, said yes. The pub lunches became our habit when we were both in the office at the same time.

My work was challenging but I enjoyed every minute of it. JBCMC's (the Jeddah Joint Venture) productivity issues were discussed with their General Manager detailing areas for improvement. One of the biggest issues there was the multicultural, multilingual workforce. This, more than anything had a huge effect on communication and work activities. Following in depth discussions with personnel working in each department and from a different country and background, I learned that, in order to understand exactly what a person means to say, a question, to confirm this, must be asked in three different ways.

A hierarchy existed where the British supervisors and managers were perceived and felt superior to the others. Indeed, as I had experienced in the UK, when some English people dealt with a foreigner, they impart a feeling of, "you know little and I am much better." The inability of that non-native person to speak, or communicate in the same way, indicates ineptitude. Obviously, there were similar feelings between other nationalities and cultures.

The staff had a number of conflicting feelings when dealing with their supervisors. They, sometimes, did not understand what exactly they were asked to do, or that they did not know how to complete a task. They were frightened that they may say or do something that will upset their superiors, leaving them at risk of punishment, or even worse, dismissal. The result of these mixed feelings, together with imperfect language and cultural understanding, rendered them feeling vulnerable and unable to question anything; instead, they just nodded their heads, implying apprehension. The supervisors and managers acted as if they were working back home, with the same foreigners who lived and worked with them.

Following further training of the supervisors and managers related to communication, emphasising cultural influences, morale and efficiency improved tremendously. Necessary reporting from the joint venture was, also, made accurately and promptly. More time could then be found to pursue the main part of my role, whilst continuing to monitor performance of both Saudi companies.

Regarding the 'business development' role, several countries with potential to invest were identified. My next step was to seek and approach suitable partners with whom we can establish new joint ventures. To achieve this, travel dominated my time. I flew to several countries including Morocco, Tunisia, Algeria, Egypt, the Gulf and Indian Sub-continent. When my flight lasted over six hours, company policy dictated First class travel. My first trip to Delhi, in India, was on an Air India 747 plane, which left Heathrow at 9pm. I was ushered to the spacious seats at the front of the plane, on the main deck, where the usual refreshments, followed by an exotic, Indian, meal were served.

Following the entertainment, I was asked if I would like to 'retire.' As it was about my bedtime, I said yes and was taken to the upper deck. Unlike the Virgin Atlantic plane, the chairs had been arranged completely flat and made up for use as beds. I was asked if I would like a hot drink, or anything else, and informed that I would be woken up about an hour before breakfast. The blinds were down and the lights switched off.

After breakfast and the plane landing, I was guided to the first-class lounge. There I was able to shower and dress for a day's meetings. I guess it saved a night at a hotel and allowed a full working day! Good for both the company, and me.

A car was waiting outside the airport building, provided by the owner of a beer company, to deliver me to him and, later, take me to the hotel. The offices were very lavish and portrayed a professional, wealthy organisation. The owner, who was also the chairman, was waiting for me in his palatial office, adorned with paintings, statues, and a fantastic silk carpet. He was wearing a very smart outfit, which included a beige Nehru jacket and linen trousers. This was a man with a net worth of over ten million pounds, looking and acting very humble and modest.

After discussions about the purpose of my visit, information about his company's activities, the country's socioeconomic status, and the beverage industry, he called his Vice President and introduced me to him. I expressed interest in looking around the facilities and was taken on a tour. Apart from the admin building and offices, I was taken to the brewery and the bottling plant, where the beer was filled and placed in crates, ready for shipment. It was a very impressive operation, not too dissimilar to those in Europe or the United States.

Following my return to the office, I was asked to join the two gentlemen for lunch in what appeared to be an exclusive dining room within the president's wing. We spent three hours eating, drinking, and talking. The owner was very open to a joint venture with us, producing cans for his beers and the rest of the carbonated beverage products. I was dropped off at the Hilton hotel and promised to keep in touch, informing them of my research, analysis, and decision regarding progression to the next stage.

Four days of visits with Government personnel, business leaders and institutions, concluded with a free day and a half. One of my hosts offered me a car with a driver to take me to the Taj Mahal. Having spent the day there, pondering its splendour, I was left with half a day to further explore Delhi before travelling to the airport for the return journey back home. This had been the first of four trips to the region; one to Bombay and Bangalore, another to Calcutta, and the fourth to Dhaka in Bangladesh. Each area had its charms, but all revealed a class system that differentiated significantly between people. The majority were very poor and about 10% extremely rich and powerful, living in luxurious homes, driving top European cars, and frequenting country clubs unattainable for the majority.

After ten months of travel around the regions and a period of further research and analysis, I was in a position to write a report, recommending the preferred course of action. It nominated a partner, supplying personal and business financial status. The country's socio-economic position and stability were also detailed in the report, together with the size of the investment, financial projections of the proposed investments and predicted return.

Three options were given. The preferred one with the Indian beer company, and two in Egypt; one producing beverage cans and the other, HDPE containers for engine oil. The latter was to be a joint venture with a well-known international oil company. All three would yield an exceptional return on investment and fantastic growth opportunities. Having delved deeper into each country's stability, probability of investment success and Government incentives, two countries were chosen, each with a very solid partner who was most likely to work well with us, and assist us in achieving a successful, profitable, business. Further negotiations with the chosen partners led to due diligence resulting in a final report, recommending that we go ahead with the investments. I had achieved my objectives in all areas. Now, it was a matter of waiting for the final go-ahead before implementation could be put into progress.

Two months later my boss asked me to join him in his office. He informed me that the parent company was to be sold. No buyer had been found, but he was concerned that there may be a need for only one of us in any new company. He then said, "One of us will have to go, and it is not going to be me." It was not yet known exactly when the sale of the company would be agreed. However, in order to ensure I left, he gave me two options. If I had been prepared to leave straight away, I would get two months' tax-free salary. However, if I decided to stay, I would work for the next two months and get paid normally, with tax deducted, and then leave with no further payments.

A couple of years after the initial conversation, significant successes under my belt and a good rapport with my manager, I found myself to be in the same position – him informing me that we could not work together. I was distraught and believed that all his action was motivated by him feeling threatened by me. It became clear that, when he had informed Head Office, in Chicago, that he wanted to dismiss me after only just over a month after joining, they asked to see and assess me first. Obviously, as I felt, they had concluded that I was the right choice, capable, showed potential and furthermore liked me; they forced him to keep me. He had finally been handed an excuse to protect his survival by ensuring my demise.

A couple of days after the announcement, Darren and I had another discussion, where he suggested that perhaps I could go to work for JBCMC in Saudi, as they were eager to have me. Again, the roller coaster had reached bottom and started to rise. There was a recession looming and it would be very difficult to get another job. I knew that he would never let me stay until the company was sold and risk being chosen as his replacement. I accepted, asking him to let them know of my willingness to joining them. This may have been the silver lining in the cloud.

Reprieve Or Reward

The General Manager of JBCMC called to say that he would love to have me on board. He offered me £48,000 tax-free per year, plus a company car, villa in a compound with a swimming pool, tennis courts, green spaces, clubs, all utilities paid for, and two return business class tickets to the UK every year. However, when he asked the Saudi Partner, who had majority shares, he was told that as I was born in Egypt, they would pay me only half of this salary and basic accommodation. I would be given £25,000 per annum, small flat and a single economy class ticket to the UK per year. Not even a company car. I was appalled and remembered how my father must have felt when we arrived in Libya, 30 years ago! Obviously I refused and, resigned to my fate, left the Windsor office effective immediately and started looking for other opportunities.

After a couple of months, I got a job as a Financial Advisor with Allied Dunbar, offering insurance and investments to the general public. I was paid commission only and had to make several cold calls to arrange appointments. For every thirty calls that I made, I managed to get an appointment. Once the appointment was made, I would make a sale. However, I hated the rude replies I received from 70% of the people I telephoned and continued to look for work. A recession had started and its grip was tightening. I had no luck; not even an interview.

Over the next six months, I had written and sent over 30 CVs, attended outsource interviews, sponsored by the department of employment, given personality and aptitude tests and

more. Finally, I was given an appointment with a person specialising in recruitment. He carried out several other tests, reviewed
the results of the previous tests undertaken and questioned me
on several topics, finding out more about me. Following all this,
he was impressed with what he thought were excellent qualifications, skills, and experiences, and believed that I was a "very
intelligent, presentable gentleman, with excellent communicating skills." He continued to emphasise that my technical, commercial, and financial ability and work experience were much
higher and more diverse than most. What puzzled him was why
I had not been asked for even one interview.

Then came the bombshell. "Would you consider changing
your name?" he asked. He felt that, because I was born in Egypt,
and despite having British Nationality, the picture of me after
seeing my name could be of a bearded [perhaps Islamist] person
who did not speak English well and had possibly made the CV
up. "Seeing you and talking to you as I now have," he continued, "I would hire you without hesitation."

Needless to say, I was shocked, but not surprised, and thanked
him for his advice, but I would continue to use my existing
name. I had suspected, experienced, and felt discriminated against
throughout my working life in England. But, on that day, it was
spelt out for me and confirmed. I was in a whirlpool, pulled down
into the dark deep abyss, with complete hopelessness. Although
England was my home and, after over twenty years, I understood
the way of life and was used to its familiarity, I was not respected
for my abilities and experiences. I was no more than a 'bloody
foreigner,' trapped, unable to escape this injustice. My excellent,
qualifications, experience and skills were negated due to my ra-
cial origin. The high paying, prestigious positions achieved by
my English born counterparts were out of reach. I had to be happy with the lesser ones available to high achieving people with
less skills, qualifications, or experience than I had. Perhaps that
was why, at that time, capable non-native personnel opted for
their own humble businesses. They would get the challenge they
yearned, which would lead to the wealth they were not allowed.

I continued as best as I could, until, shortly afterwards, to my surprise, I received a phone call from the Financial Manager working with the Saudi partner of my ex-company. He informed me that Sheikh AKS wanted me to work with them, and was prepared to pay me whatever I wanted, give me 'compound' accommodation of my choice and two business class return flights between London and Saudi Arabia per annum if I joined them at JBCMC. After agreeing to all the terms, including a healthy £58,000 tax-free salary, fully expensed Volvo car and all utilities for the accommodation paid, I moved to Jeddah in June of 1992. I remember thinking, "There is a God out there."

On my arrival, I was informed that my ex-boss, who was still the Area GM for the new company, which acquired the old CCC, in which I worked, objected. He did not want me to take this senior position. As the Saudi partner owned 51% of the shares, he had the final say. He had informed my boss, in no uncertain terms, that he must give me a senior post within the Joint Venture with at least the terms agreed by him. If he did not do this, he would replace the existing General Manager with me. Needless to say, I was accepted and given the title of Commercial Manager, reporting to the GM of JBCMC and responsible for Sales & Marketing, Purchasing & Warehousing and Distribution. I understood, later on, that the Saudi partner was planning to set up a can making company in Egypt and that he hoped that I would do it for him.

After the first year, despite many challenges, I was very pleased with what I achieved. Material and distribution costs were significantly reduced, the first ever company brochure was designed and produced, on a very tight budget, and by introducing international customers, sales were increased, from a maximum 750 million cans per year, to a record of one billion cans. Company efficiency and profitability was the best it had ever been. I had worked hard and ensured that I kept the partner informed of the strategy and execution.

The GM, initially frightened for his position, was persuaded that my intentions were not to compete with him, but to help in transforming the company of which he was the head, to the success that he could boast about. Socially, I spent a good deal of time with him and other senior colleagues in our compounds. We held parties, dinners, lunches, and social events, during weekends and non-working hours, played tennis and arranged swimming events. As alcohol was not allowed in Saudi, we would purchase non-alcoholic beer from the supermarket, again, within the compound, buy extra sugar and yeast, and produce the alcoholic drinks. Also, in groups, we would take 4X4 SUV's and explore sites in the dessert. It was an incredible life, albeit somewhat artificial. However, I vowed I would advise any young couple, or family, to seek international work and live as expatriates. The cultural exposure and experience would not only increase their knowledge and skills, but also their outlook on life and communicating skills. Through exposure to different nationalities – how they live, work and act – better understanding of people in general develops, as does lateral thinking and problem-solving abilities.

Two and a half years later, I was offered a fantastic challenge to assist in the start up of a beverage can manufacturing company in Egypt. It was a $40M project, creating the first such company in North Africa. I went back to the UK and, from there, moved to Cairo, Egypt, in 1996.

Egypt, for me, was unlike any other country in which I worked. Although I was born and lived my first six years there, I had been transformed by our travels and living in Western countries. Despite prejudices that plagued me during my career, I related more to the British way of life and Western way of doing business. Here, achievement was only possible through, not only very hard work but, more so, dependent on knowing the right contacts. Everything was incredibly bureaucratic until you manage to get to that right person, at the right level, making the seemingly impossible, possible.

At the time, there did not appear to be a sense of pride available, amongst some people, in the work they produce. It was like getting the basic finish to anything, without caring about the quality. A factory, for example, would be poorly finished with undulating floors and walls, basically plastered or painted, and full of imperfections. Toilets were basic, with pipes and cables running along the walls, without any attempt to hide them. When having our factory built, our concerns about the finish, resulted in the response, "You did not ask for a five-star hotel!" Hard work and close supervision, together with penalty clauses in the contract, forced the completion of a 'five-star' manufacturing building, grounds, and interior. Plant and machinery were installed and commissioned and finally, the offices and commercial spaces were ready to be occupied.

Every step taken to progress the start-up was met with resistance. It quickly became apparent that a great deal of corruption existed, with a lot of 'under the table' bribes being the norm, and necessary in order to lubricate progression. I could, and indeed, later, did employ and send a person to complete these routines and deal with appropriate governmental personnel. Also, I could have telephoned contacts in high places and, what would take days, or even weeks, would be concluded immediately.

I wanted to learn how things worked and experience the processes directly. An application needed to be made to a government organisation in the 6th of October District, where the factory was built. To achieve this, I decided to personally visit their offices, as an ordinary worker. When I got there, I enquired about what to do and where to go. First, I was sent to an office upstairs, where I paid some fees for the application. This was followed by a trip back downstairs and along a corridor to another office where I collected the form. I was then directed to a second building where I climbed more stairs and walked through corridors to wait my turn to sit with an employee who would check and complete the form and stamp it. I was apparently lucky on that day; I only had to wait an hour. Having completed this stage of the process, I was sent to the original building for final signature and stamp, before the final completion of the process. Apart from the good exercise and enlightenment, I spent over two hours to complete this seemingly simple mission.

This and many other similar escapades led me to writing articles in the Newspapers, highlighting the immense hardship people went through to achieve what should be a fairly simple and straightforward task. For my first encounter, I asked why the process could not start and finish at the same location, leaving all the requirements being completed in the background. That is, an applicant is directed to a window where he would collect the form and complete it (or bring the completed form with him/her). Having handed the form into the appropriate window, the applicant would then sit and wait for everything to be authorised, requiring only that he collect this from the window before departing. It is all about saving energy, dignity, and time. Of course, it would be ideal if all this could have been done by mail, or even digitally (though that would not be possible then).

After the administrative work of setting up the company's operations was complete, I turned my attention to the acquisition of customers. Before I could approach anyone, I had to establish the total costs of production, recommend, and agree with the partners, an acceptable mark-up, recommend an initial price to encourage and grow sales, agree on the availability of cans and, finally, identification and negotiations with potential businesses. Our potential customers were divisions of multinational companies, such as Pepsi Cola, Coca Cola and Schweppes. Through discussions with the heads of the companies, the first obstacle was to persuade them to invest in a new filling line especially for the filling of the beverages into cans. The general public would also have to be persuaded to buy canned, instead of bottled, beverages, and pay the premium. A great deal of time wining and dining was necessary to facilitate negotiations and final agreement. The representative of one customer insisted that he should be taken to the most expensive sushi restaurant in Cairo. Bargaining was a way of life and required a special strategy in negotiating.

Agreements reached had to be fulfilled. The quality of the can had to be to an exact specification with no compromise. The supply of necessary material and distribution of finished goods was equally important. Sounds easy? Not in Egypt at the time. It proved to be the most challenging period in my working life. Correct employee availability, training, and dealings with

Governmental departments, was very time consuming, frustrating, and extremely exhausting.

I had to ensure the best material required for production at the lowest costs. Approximately 90% of this was purchased from abroad. The main stock in the production of our cans was the coiled steel, which formed the main body. Over the years, sourcing it proved to be a very interesting and challenging occupation. Several steel producers around the world were eager to supply us. A couple of years after start, our annual contract was worth over $100 million. Suppliers were desperate to gain the business and I was determined to reduce its costs. One company decided to offer me a one-million-dollar bribe if I signed the contract with them. Having already negotiated the price to the lowest possible, I decided, to their extreme surprise, that this should be passed onto the company and forced them to give us a further 10% reduction instead of giving it to me personally.

Clearing customs was a nightmare. Duty was payable on all imported material and a tremendous amount of effort was needed to ensure the correct duties were paid and clearance occurs without delay. However, as the whole world was about to implement 'free trade' customs tariffs, there were certain products that became exempt from duty. Unfortunately, most of our supplies were not included in this and, sadly, the products we produced attracted a very small tariff when imported from abroad. This, during the early stages of manufacture, resulted in other international companies being able to import beverage cans into Egypt, at a lower cost than we could offer.

It became obvious that, if this were to continue, we would not survive. After many discussions with several senior government personnel, I was unable to get anywhere. Eventually, I managed to establish contact with the, then, Prime Minister. I explained the situation; that being a newly established company, our costs were high and that should we not get support, we would have no alternative than to shut down. The result of this would be unemployment for our staff and employees and no tax from the income we would have produced, to the country. We must have some 'barrier to trade' for both the country's benefits and ours. Following this, a levy was introduced on any beverage cans imported into the country. We now had a fighting chance of survival. Within four years we had quadrupled sales, supplying cans for the beer, as well as the beverage industry in Egypt and overseas.

Socially, my wife, daughter and I lived the lives of kings and queens. My wife worked as a very Senior Manager in the regional office of a large oil company. Both of us commanded huge incomes and benefits. We resided in an affluent suburb, east of Cairo, had properties on the north cost, including a chalet in Ballah, a beachfront resort on the Mediterranean Sea, and a villa at Stella Di Mari, on the Red Sea. We were members of the best three clubs in Cairo; the exclusive Qutameya Heights golf and country club, and the Gezira and Heliopolis Sporting clubs. All of them boasted several swimming pools, gyms, spas, tennis and squash courts, restaurants and cafeterias, and internal lounges for adults only use. The first two had golf courses, with Gezira also boasting a horseracing track with stables.

Most weekends and long holidays were spent in our villa in Stella Di Mari. Our family and friends would join us and enjoy swimming in the Red Sea, or a large ornamental pool shared between eight villas. In the evenings, we would visit one of several restaurants, or hold parties with music, food, and drinks, lasting to the early hours of the morning. For those inclined, a game of tennis or golf putting could be played during the day.

During the summer months, we would travel to the north coast to escape the heat and humidity of Cairo. Similar pursuits were followed as in Stella, only this time, they were held along the Mediterranean coastline. Our house, together with our neighbours', were always open to everyone during these times. It was wonderful, made easier by the availability of each family's domestic help for the duration of the stay.

There were several invitations to parties at private events and the British embassy. One of the events organised by our company was the millennium celebration at the Pyramids. Several tents were laid out with bars and dining tables, allowing guests to eat, drink, socialise and watch a musical light show displayed on the Pyramids. Another was an invitation to the British ambassador's residence. There, people from different countries, wearing lavish clothing, traditional to their own customs, attended and mixed, encouraging global interaction… and a few drinks!

I remember we were invited to a party where several celebrities and members of the elite social class were gathered. At one point we were walking through from one room to another, when I turned to find one of my favourite actresses, coming up from behind me. I instinctively stopped, held my arm out, beckoning her through. As she reached me, I could not help but put my hand on her waist and guide her through. She looked at me and smiled, allowing me to talk to her, voicing my immense admiration of her and her acting. Unfortunately, my wife asked me to join her to meet and greet some other friends and acquaintances.

One day I received a phone call from a head-hunter, looking for a Director of Operations for a 250-bed private hospital. He had heard about me and what I had achieved thus far, and felt that I would be ideal for the position. Apparently, a doctor, who had spent his life working with the royal family in Saudi, acquired it for his son. The hospital had previously been taken over by the banks after its board of directors embezzled all its profits and absconded with millions of pounds in cash. The new owner employed a medical doctor as the Medical Director and an English Chief Executive Officer. I would report to the CEO, responsible for all the non-medical parts of the hospital. My brief was to return the hospital to a truly international position, which it had reached in its successful days.

I always relish a challenge and, after a couple of meetings with the agent and CEO, I was persuaded by an offer which was more than double my current salary. At the time, my wife and I had purchased a plot of land in Obour city and wanted to build our dream home on it. It was estimated to cost about one million pounds. Whereas our savings would have been barely enough, the extra income would help ensure that we build and furnish it exactly as we wanted. As ECANCO, the can making company, was now firmly on its feet and successful, and the MD would not offer better benefits in recognition of the huge profits being made, I could not refuse the proposal and new position.

When I joined the hospital, I discovered corruption, incompetence, inefficiency, and very poor standards throughout the organisation. More importantly, the finance department did not have a Financial Manager and had not produced financial results and documents for approximately three years. Although there was an IT department, it was very poorly, if at all, utilised. Hundreds of thousands of pounds of customer care software, purchased three years earlier, had not been used. Maintenance was all but non-existent. Repair was on-demand, if and when it was requested. Much work was needed to bring it to an acceptable state before achieving the 'international' objective.

Having discussed these failings with all the heads of departments, it was obvious that much needed to be done. Training courses were provided to improve their supervisory and management ability. To speed up the process, I personally, developed and delivered several training sessions, based on each manager's needs. An IT Manager with good experience was employed and the suppliers of the 'Customer Care' software were asked to attend to ensure the efficient functionality of their applications. I took personal charge of the accounting department and started gathering figures related to all the financial transactions of the business. Finally, financial statements for the previous three years were produced. We were able to invite Coopers and Lybrand to attend, audit and approve our books and financial position, and give advice and guidance to acquiring a first-class financial control structure and department. We were on our way to achieving a successful business.

In one year, corruption was cremated, costs were significantly reduced, the operations were fully computerised, and financial control was resurrected and fully developed. Patients' records were integrated into a hospital-wide network system, starting with appointments, accommodations, treatments, medications, Nursing, Doctor interventions, discharge and billing could all be viewed at the touch of a button. Maintenance was carried out according to a schedule, with repairs given priority depending on health and safety. Communication was knowledge, power, and control; we now had all that.

One day, the Purchasing Manager asked me if I could talk to the Sales Director of a supplier. We had asked for a quote to supply new electronic, multi-positional beds. After discussion about the value of the contract and some price negotiations, we reached a figure of £380,000, which I was not ready to accept. The director lowered his voice, although there was only him and I in my office, and whispered, "We will give you 15% of this value if you accept this quote and give us the order."

I had been through several of these 'under the table' offers and knew he meant to offer me a £57,000 'incentive' for accepting the purchase. No one would know. I looked at him, confirmed my understanding, smiled and said "OK, done! You will reduce the price by a further £57,000, leaving the total for the beds at £323,000. I will ask our purchasing department to send you an order, as agreed, for that amount." This had not been the first, nor the last time during my working career that I had been offered bribes to expedite acquisitions. I could never accept such deceit to my employer. The salary I had accepted for taking the job prevented me from taking an extra penny that could reduce the company's profitability for my benefit.

Within two years, costs in the hospital had been reduced by over 30%, quality and professionalism was high, and there were more patients than ever before. Our reputation was truly 'International'. However, the owner was a 28-year-old doctor who had recently graduated and was more interested in glamour and the pursuit of social pleasures. His father, who bought him the hospital, died and an uncle, who had been a General in the army, was 'helping' him run it. It quickly became clear that he was only interested in increasing his own personal wealth and securing a very comfortable retirement. I had been instructed to deposit £1M per month into his bank account. The owner appeared to know this, and was happy for it to happen. I was careful and warned them of the legal and auditable implications of doing something like that. The General was not happy and did not accept my advice.

The General was a slim man in his late fifties to very early sixties. He was obviously used to giving orders and expecting total, unquestioned obedience. People in his employment were considered as slaves with rights that he alone might decide to give them. It was a relationship of 'master-slave' between him and the hospital employees. Even my boss, the CEO, didn't get on with him and avoided any unnecessary close dealings.

I was looking for a Finance Manager and one day, the General and I had a discussion about the outcome of the interviews and, in particular, a person whom he introduced and wanted to be hired. Unfortunately, having reviewed the candidate's CV, discussed his previous work with him and tested his claimed knowledge and experience, I concluded that he was not the right person for the job. The discussion with the General turned into a shouting match, with him treating me, for the first time, in the same way he treats other staff. I could not accept this, informed him of my feelings and walked out. I had helped to raise the hospital from almost total failure to its newly acquired status of a truly well run, good quality, successful International hospital. He wanted his own Finance Manager in position, I felt, to drain the cash into his pockets. I wanted to strengthen the hospital further by building the best and most qualified personnel.

I learned that, apart from anything else, he had acquired a property at the Qutameya Heights club, of which I was a member. He needed at least £4M to complete the purchase and bring it to the size and condition he wanted it to be. It was because of him and his unquenchable thirst for money, that I decided I could not continue my work there.

From a mixture of our salaries, savings, and past investments, we had built a huge villa that, at the time, was the envy of most people. It was built on a plot measuring 1300 square metres and included a large garden, swimming pool with a waterfall feature, dressing room and a three-story house on a 350 square metre footprint. The basement included a spare bedroom, large leisure space, a maids' quarters, with its bathroom and kitchen, a double garage and a self-contained Porter's accommodation. The ground floor housed a large kitchen-breakfast area, above average walk-in larder, guest cloakroom and a good size hanging space for guests' coats and the like. The entrance was reached via marble steps with columns supporting a roof, an oval stained-glass window and handmade double doors, carved of oak, depicting a woven cloth. It was a grand entrance, covering a space of 25 square metres. Inside was a small indoor garden with leaded base and sides and planted with plants and a couple of small trees. I had an office with its own terrace and steps leading into the garden. There was a huge guest reception room, a dining room and steps leading down to our living room. Through sliding doors there was a patio, covered with a pergola and overlooking the gardens and swimming pool. The glass in the reception room doors and living room partition was decoratively engraved. A square staircase led down to the basement and up to the first floor and roof area. The banisters were designed and made of decorative steel with oak handrails. On the first floor was a guest wing with a bedroom, bathroom, and kitchenette, as well as my wife's study and daughter's bedroom – both sharing a balcony. Our sleeping quarters, on the same floor, comprised a huge bedroom with seating area and balcony, a walk-in dressing room with wardrobes, and an en-suite with two basins set in a marble top, the toilet and shower both partitioned using glass bricks. There was also a two-person Jacuzzi in one corner. The roof space housed a room, water tank and three 1.5 metre satellite dishes, pointing in different directions. There was a tiled floor and a decorative sloping tiled roof around the house.

The external gates and garage door were IR controlled, operated by us when we arrived, or left the property. We employed a security firm, who placed guards in a wooden-built room outside, on duty 24 hours a day. There was a porter with his wife staying in the quarters built for them, and two maids and a nanny for our daughter living and working within the premises. As the house was so big, and built of thick concrete and brick walls, we needed 24 telephone extensions to facilitate communications. There were music speakers in every room and video intercom between the main entrance and several places where there will always be someone. We had achieved our 'Dream house!' My father saw the land before anything was built. Sadly, he did not see it completed. When I had taken him to the site, he thought that I was crazy to have bought land in the middle of the desert.

A couple of years earlier, my parents were living in our house in England. My wife, while on a business trip from Cairo, went to stay with them for a couple of days. My father was about to travel to Egypt and, as he was leaving the house, gave her his keys saying, "Loufi, take these, I will not be needing them again." I saw him in Cairo and felt as if he was making a point to talk to, see and meet everyone he knew. It was as if he was saying good-bye.

In two weeks, he accompanied me to gatherings with friends and relatives, saw the flat I was temporarily living in before our house was built, and spent time reminiscing about the past. He would ask me to pour myself a drink or three, and confess, "I want to make you talk without barricades." I heard about his achievements and regrets, particularly during our childhood. Expressing pride in all that I had achieved, he asked me to look after my mother, brothers, and sister when he is gone. Shocked at his comment, I scolded him for even thinking about that and that I hoped he would be with us for a long time to come.

We had a disagreement about something he said about my mother, and I left, not wanting to speak to him again. Three days later, I decided to call and make it up with him. He sounded happy, chatted for a while, and then asking when he would see me. I was busy at work and replied by saying, "I am really not sure when we will be able to meet." On Friday, first day of the weekend, I called him, but had no reply. I tried a couple of times and still no response. My nephews' cousins called me to say that they were supposed to have been going out with my father. However, when they went to collect him, he did not open the door and appeared not to be there.

I became worried, called a doctor friend of mine and asked him to join me immediately, as my father was not responding to anyone. As we approached the flat in Zamalek, the bedroom window was open. I felt slightly relieved, thinking that he was OK. We parked the car and, as I was rushing up the stairs and towards the flat, I feared the worst, but tried to think positively. When we got to the entrance, I rang the doorbell. There was no reply. I rang again and tried to unlock it, only to find it had been bolted on the inside. Shouting, "Baba (dad), open the door!" I knocked harder, forcing the neighbours to come out to see what was happening. I held the key in the open position of the lock and with my shoulder, pushed it violently until it broke open.

The flat was dark and silent, as none of the shutters had been opened. Shouting Baba, Baba, I ran through the reception area to the corridor, when I saw the door into his bedroom closed. The adrenaline forced my heart to race and warning me of danger. I ran and tried to open the door, again shouting Baba. The door was bolted from the inside and there was no sound from within. I broke it, ran though a small corridor and there he was, sitting on his chair, underneath the open window. In shock, I called him, but he did not move. He was holding a strip of pills as if about to pop one out of the blister. There was an expression of surprise on his face. As I approached him, I knew he had gone.

MV, my doctor friend, came into the room, examined him, and confirmed my worst fear. I tried very hard to control my emotions and stop the tears from streaming down my cheeks. We lifted his body and placed it on the bed, ensuring, as MV insisted, that the head be facing East. He was still in his seated form. I knew that at this time, more than ever before, I could no longer control my emotions. MV saw this and said that he would go to the department of health and prepare the necessary paperwork. I walked out behind him and found the reception room full of people. Uncontrollably I shouted at them, asking them to leave. I did not want anyone to see me lose control, so closed the door and walked back into the bedroom.

Seeing him there, motionless, I could no longer stop a flood of tears, crying loudly in response to intense sadness and allowing my body to return to a state of balance. I walked over to him, bent down and kissed his forehead. I had to call my wife to tell her, but perhaps, also, bring her to my side.

The Rat Race

I had promised my wife that I would give our new life in Egypt several years to decide if I wanted to stay permanently. After seven years, I started to question many things about the way of life in the country. I loved our friends and relatives, the life we lived, with membership of the three best clubs, great cars, drivers, household staff and what seemed an enormous amount of money to do almost anything we wanted to. Still, I kept asking "who's in heaven and who's in hell?"

Life for people in Egypt at that time was a matter of fending for oneself. Corruption was rife and it appeared as if no one cared about the country as a whole. Individuals had to fight hard for what they wanted; even needed. Government employees were given a meagre salary, impossible to sustain a family, whilst people with power, influence, and money, along with those that managed to place themselves within these people's circles, found ways around the system. The less able employees in government offices had to get more money from somewhere. The easiest way to do this was to make the general public pay for any request made. It became openly known that if one needed something done, which may well be their right, one would have to pay, 'under the table,' over and above the publicised fee payable. The poor and most vulnerable, the majority of the population, had to do this, or wait a long time to conclude their business. They were very likely to be sent on a run-around across the city to different offices, only to find, eventually, that they would return and pay to get the job done. The more well-off sent someone else to do all this for them. The richer, more influential, and more powerful called the senior personnel, who owed them a favour, or had been given generous contributions in the past, and asked them to intervene, expediting the request. I, along with a great many senior managers/owners, had to do this all the time, something I really disliked.

The sad thing was that, unless you were rich and powerful, it was very, very difficult to get your rights. For example, the personnel who were supposed to read the utility meters to generate the monthly bill, may decide to do another, better paying job, in parallel to their Government's main employment. The result of this was that they did not always get actual readings. A fictitious figure is then given to the appropriate office for processing. A consumer must then pay the demanded amount, even if it was much higher than it should have been, before they could dispute it. Then, it's a waiting game until, or if, they get their money back. More often than not, it was almost impossible to find a responsible manager to complain to.

I remember one day I was walking down a street approaching one of the embassies. It was in the evening and the area was very quiet. A constable carrying a rifle came out of his guardroom and approached me. I was shocked to find him asking for money "to buy some tea!" This was not only unfortunate, but also dangerous. Firstly, the fact that he had a weapon could be interpreted as threatening – "I have a rifle, if you don't give me money…" Secondly, what was to stop someone from offering him a modest amount of money (which, to him, might appear a great deal), to allow him into the embassy, or ask him to place a bomb into its grounds?

The infrastructure was basic. Roads, pavements, pipework, electricity, all were of very poor-quality material and workmanship. Again, the need for more money, forced the responsible people to take bribes and accept poor-quality material and shoddy work. It had become a part of life, inescapable for most. Things did not improve that much in the time that I was there. No one seemed to be held accountable, pushing all to use force and aggression to get anything close to what they really needed. Traffic was abysmal, with an 'everything goes' attitude. The poor, sometimes conscripted, soldiers were not supported. It would be disastrous for one of them to stop a person flouting the traffic laws, lest they turn out to be rich or powerful citizens, some important politician, or their children. It was likely for that recruit to be relocated to somewhere, miles away from his family and in the worst part of the country.

I was a prisoner in a palace, not enjoying the lack of environmental excellence outside. Then, I wondered if quantity really was more important than quality. Eventually, after a three-week visit to one of my best friends in Melbourne, Australia, my wife and I decided to go for quality. My friend had tried to persuade us to join them there. However, after much thought and discussions it became clear that we already had roots, and were much more familiar with somewhere else. We decided to move back to England.

The next important thing to consider was that of employment. Would I be able to get a job there? In the past, it had become very difficult. Not only had it been concluded by an agent that my chances would improve if I changed my name, but, also, before having been given the job in Saudi, I had been turned down for all the senior roles to which I had applied. There was always "...someone with experience, or skills...more appropriate..." Now, with the extra experience, knowledge and exposure gained, I would be applying for even more senior roles. I tried by applying to a couple of positions, which I felt were very suitable and sought individuals who had very slightly less than I can offer. Sadly, I received the same rejection letters as in the past. I had attached an incredible reference, given by my English CEO in Egypt, to the CV and covering letter sent. What more could I have done?

This led to a lot of soul searching and questioning about how other non-native English people felt about not been given suitable senior positions. My mind took me to the like of a 'corner shop' and similar small businesses. Most of these were owned and run by Indians, Pakistanis, or other ethnic minorities. A good many of them had succeeded and became very wealthy. During the nineties, I believe I heard that there were 100 millionaires called Patel. Most of these people had been denied the chance to prove their abilities in companies within the UK. Their frustration and lack of challenge forced them into becoming self-employed. Their families helped them, financially, contributing to their start-ups. Perhaps employment was not the answer for me.

I had convinced myself not to consider working for an employer and to move out of the rat race. Perhaps all I needed was a small business, providing a modest income, whilst at the same time, not overly stretching. After all, I thought, I did not really need such a high income.

In 2003, after searching through a number of different going concerns, I chose one, which appeared to yield a very good return on investment. I started a company and called it Shorelife Limited, operating in the retail and management services industries. The name of it was to reflect its location, which was by the coast. The chosen business, which would be purchased by the company, was a Newsagent, with a Sub Post Office, in my preferred part of the country, the Southeast. Shoreham-by-Sea was a quaint town on the southern coast of West Sussex, with a direct train service into London taking just over an hour and a quarter.

We bought a four-bedroom house on Shoreham Beach, which was five minutes' walk from the Post Office, on a peninsula bounded by the river Adur on the north side and the sea to the south. It was much smaller than our 'Dream house' in Egypt, forcing us to sell or give away over half of the furniture we had, before shipping the rest to it. Our belongings were delivered in two 20-foot containers, blocking the road on arrival. Our house in Egypt was put up for sale, but did not sell for a number of years. The only way for us to purchase the property in Shoreham was to acquire a loan, or mortgage, to keep us going until the one in Cairo was sold.

The close proximity to the shop was excellent, as I had to get there at five o'clock in the morning to sort out the newspapers, ready for delivery. My wife, having left a high-powered job, decided not to have anything to do with the business, in order to pursue her passion: art. The shop opened at 6:30 and the Post Office at 9:00, which meant that I had to hire an assistant to look after the shop whilst I ran the post office.

At first, it was exciting and somewhat challenging. Post Office Limited (POL) had given me training, at their training centre, prior to opening and during the first couple of weeks after taking over the business. They allocated a member of their training staff to ensure that I understood the operations necessary and performed it correctly and well. The post office comprised only one counter and I considered to be very small with limited expansion. It occupied an area approximately two metres square at the back right hand corner of the newsagents' shop. It was isolated via two floor-to-ceiling partitions, made of wooden frames with steel painted panels covering the bottom half and toughened glass sealing the upper half. At the front, there was a serving hatch, as well as an opening window for collecting large items. A secure door, with a lock, was fitted to the side, accessible via the back of the main shop counter. The shop itself measured approximately 6x8 metres, plus a service area at the back, approximately 3x8 metres, with a door to the car park and delivery area. The frontage of the shop was well lit, with glass rising from 75cm above the ground up to the ceiling. A glass door in the middle provided the entrance to the premises.

Within six months, I had gained enough experience to allow me to run the business fairly easily. I organised my time such that I could spend it running the Post Office, carry out the purchasing of stock for the shop, attending to administrative and staff matters and ensuring cashflow was good for both company and household expenses. When balancing the books for the Post Office, there were the odd occasions when there would be a discrepancy. However, after unsuccessful discussions with Head Office, I put it down to mistakes due to little experience. At the time, I could not see the catastrophic events yet to come!

Soon, looking at the real standard of living and our expenses, I realised that the income from the shop and office was less than expected. More importantly, I must admit, I was, also, getting a little bit bored and needed more challenge. After some thought, research, and analysis, I discovered that larger Post Offices needed relief Postmasters to help with staff shortages. These offices were very much bigger than mine, and would enable me to learn and experience, not only from their extended product range, but, also, other, related business operations and management. To facilitate this, I hired an assistant to run my Post Office and help with the shop. The salary I was able to pay her, left me with a positive income after my earnings from the relief work. It was only for a couple of days a week and, with the Post Office closing on Wednesdays and Saturday afternoons, together with Sundays, left me enough time for other necessary work and financial issues. Also, I had time to offer other business services and start-up advice, bringing a very modest, but much needed income.

A year later, I had learned a great deal about the Post Office and general retail. The experience confirmed to me that I needed more than just this one unit. Also, I was able to manage the existing business, through the two members of staff, well. I could now see that, coming from a very demanding career, managing multi-million-pound businesses, with their enormous stresses and challenges, this was not fulfilling enough. I was wrong in my original thoughts that opting out of the rat race would be fulfilling enough for me.

I knew that about three quarters of a mile away, on the beach, there was another Post Office. It was owned by a mature woman, in her seventies, whom I felt could be persuaded to retire. I went to visit it and investigated its performance, by observation of footfall and discussions with others familiar with the business. Buying it, would give me a monopoly on the beach, an area of approximately 10 sq. kilometres, and better economies of scale. To this end, I approached the owner, Paula, convincing her that, after over 40 years' work, the cash she would receive from its sale and revenues generated from rental of the property in which the business was run, would enable her to retire and enjoy a life of leisure.

Following our agreement, the purchase process of East Beach lasted a lot longer than expected. In the meantime, I became aware of another Post Office – Mill Lane, with a mini convenience store that was being sold. Its turnover was higher than either of the other ones. Although it was about five miles further away than the others, I could not resist its potential and decided to purchase it as well. This extra venture meant that I would have to take out a loan guaranteed by our home. Two and a half years after the purchase of the first unit, West Beach, I was managing three branches with twelve members of staff and fifteen newspaper boys and girls. I, also, decided to acquire alcohol licenses for the two new premises, whilst carrying on offering some business services, including management training and advice on new small business start-ups.

The new size of the business was very demanding, and I had to reduce the non-retail, or Post Office, part to a bare minimum. Spending over 70 hours a week working was the norm. Fortunately, I was able to employ and train good, honest, and reliable people. They worked well as a team allowing me time to do more important activities. Every year, I invited them out to good local venues, where we enjoyed a meal and drinks to celebrate Christmas.

I had never considered any life-threatening risk of running a Post Office, until it reared its ugly head. One day, I was working inside West Beach Post Office, with the door from the shop into it locked, as usual. My assistant was getting some stock for the shop out of the storeroom at the back, when the front door was violently pushed open and three hooded individuals, dressed in black, ran into the shop waving machetes and hammers. Two of them ran towards me and the third went into the back. One opened the shop till and started taking the money from within it. The other was banging on my door, shouting, "Open the door," whilst threatening me with the machete. I had activated the alarm and would not open the door. After a while, the person who had run into the back came out, holding my assistant with one hand and threatening to hit her with a hammer if I did not let them into the tiny post office. I had to open the door to save my assistant, allowing one of them to push me back, with the machete in his hand, while the other opened the drawer and took whatever money was in it. I was then asked to open the safe. Not wanting to do this, I pretended I was panicking with fright and did not know where the key was. I eventually found the key and told them that, it would take a couple of minutes after I turned it before the safe would open. I explained that it was a safety mechanism. Suddenly, they muttered something and started to run out of the store. They had decided the alarm had been ringing long enough and that the arrival of the police was imminent. POL arrived on the following day and carried out an audit, which revealed that the assailants had grabbed £1000. This, along with the £250 taken from the shop till, could have been much higher, had I not resisted opening the safe. The police interviewed my assistant and took her jumper for tests. They interviewed me in a nearby house, equipped with cameras and equipment meant for this type of interrogations. Obviously, they decided that I did not have anything to do with the robbery. However, they never found the gang.

The day-to-day operations of the Post Offices included the obvious processing of letters and packages, selling of stamps, bus tickets and other promotional products. On the financial side, we sold and cashed Postal Orders, and offered cash withdrawals and deposits facilities on behalf of other banks, investments processing for National Savings and Investment (NSI) and foreign currency transactions. I wondered why we could not offer banking facilities like any other bank. This was suggested to POL personnel but, after several unsuccessful attempts at persuading them, I could not.

Cash and stock necessary for the office was supplied by POL and all transactions in and out were entered onto a computerised system known as Horizon. At the end of each day, everything must be accounted for. Cheques, deposit slips and any other items requiring return were checked and sent to POL in a special pouch given directly to a Postman. The system, which was directly connected to Head Office, was the heart of the operation. Controlled via a touch screen and keyboard, it had attached to it several peripherals, including a set of weighing scales and a bankcard (ATM) machine.

Imagine you, as a customer, wanted to post a parcel. It would be placed onto the weighing scales, which would be detected by Horizon, which in turn, would calculate the cost of postage and print the appropriate label. Bank deposits and withdrawals are logged onto the system. Stock, including, stamps, bus tickets, cash, and others, received, or returned are also keyed into it. ATM card purchases or withdrawals are also recorded and confirmed by Horizon. Any cheques, deposit slips and other, transaction, related documents must be sealed in a specially coloured and printed pouch, and hand presented to a postman, as explained earlier. They would then be delivered to Head Office for processing. Should there be any discrepancies with the Horizon calculated information, an error message would be sent to the appropriate Post Office branch.

Following detection, POL would send a 'transaction correction,' effectively allowing the Subpostmaster to confirm this, enabling Horizon to adjust their accounts accordingly. Any shortfalls must be paid back to POL and are deducted from the Subpostmaster's monthly remunerations. Although I was allowed to dispute them, the onus was on us to disprove it. In the first few months at the smaller West Beach branch, and after several unsuccessful, or ignored, objections, I decided not to quibble much. Perhaps, I thought, the lack of experience caused these relatively small shortages, and that there would be other error messages that would compensate for them.

Cashflow Crises

In 2006, about eight months after starting the other two branches, I started receiving 'error' and 'correction' reports. There were discrepancies in the cash reported and Post Office's system records. As the income from these two offices was more than three times the original one, their shortfalls were much more substantial. Apparently, we owed them about eight thousand pounds. More importantly, the shortages were advised to us almost a year from when they were supposed to have occurred. It took me and the clerks in the offices a couple of days to dig out and look through the receipts and reports during that period. We could not interrogate the Horizon system enough to collect important and necessary detailed information. Evidence from the small slips we kept as receipts of transactions were not accepted by them as proof of system error.

Over the next few months, the analysed figures began to show that, although on the face of it there appeared to be shortages, there was something wrong that we could not understand and was not logical. One item that I had identified was to do with business deposits, which are daily takings to be passed onto the customers' respective banks following processing by Head Office.

Both cash and cheques were deposited using a single banking slip, and one possible error could have been the recording of the cash amounts and value of the cheques. The deposit slips should have the value of the cheques and the amount of cash recorded separately, with the total written on the bottom. If I, or a clerk, had inadvertently recorded the whole amount as cash, the system would show an excess of cash than would actually be available. This can easily happen and, indeed, I noticed it a couple of times during spot checks made.

This is a mistake which should not happen but is easily done. As the slips and cheques were sent to Head Office, there was no way for us to re-examine them. However, when Head Office personnel processed and verified the deposits, they, or the system should have noticed the excess value of cheque payments, or the higher amounts of cash not balancing with the cheque values. Effectively, it would have shown the actual total deposit, with a much-reduced cash value, exonerating the branch from any cash shortages.

I pointed this out to Head Office and argued that the loss was just a paper one and not actual cash. Of course, this could have been checked by Head Office and confirmed by the banks. As it had taken so long for these error messages to be sent, it made everything impossible to dispute and check. Also, POL personnel, probably, did not want to spend the time and effort in checking events that had occurred a year earlier. Furthermore, had I been allowed to scrutinise the Horizon system, I could have checked and verified it. Alas, the Subpostmasters had minimal access to their data.

Soon after this first issue, more error messages appeared. One such message reported a £300 cash shortage for a cheque, which had actually been sent to POL. It seemed that, instead of it being credited to us, the system debited it, resulting in me being charged £600. Another was 400 Euros, which were seen recorded on Horizon, only to find that, several hours later, it had mysteriously disappeared from the system; I had to pay it back. Other errors we discovered, were shortages in the coins delivered. One bag was £50 short. We were told that these bags were checked and CCTV monitored the staff filling and sealing them.

The Horizon system would report weird and unexplained transactions and results. One day, a discrepancy, yet again, appeared on the system, prompting one of the assistants to call Head Office for an explanation. He was, surprisingly, told that there was a glitch in the system and that they were working on resolving it. I wrote to Head Office again in an attempt to get a reaction and resolve these incredible shortages. In my letter I gave examples of system errors and explained that, having been an Electronics Engineer, working with IT equipment throughout my career, I had encountered many system malfunctions, software errors, corruption of data due to power outage and total system failure, resulting in loss of data. I insisted that the "losses" reported could very well have been, mostly caused by the Horizon system.

The lack of response, or complete denial that the problem may have been their fault was very disappointing and frustrating. Ironically, several months later, POL sent a letter to all Subpostmasters explaining that there had been an issue with Horizon, which caused an overpayment that, now, had to be deducted from us. We could not dispute it, as we had no way of interrogating the system.

Error messages continued to arrive until our losses amounted to some 30% of remunerations. In one year, after numerous correspondences and adjustments, I was sent an account statement for one branch, demanding £3,555.45 covering three months. There had been some, low value errors, which we accepted. However, there were no compensating notices, resulting in having to pay the majority of the debits.

There were several other issues that impacted my income through system disagreements. One of these showed how personnel within Head Office did not follow up, or deal, conscientiously with any possible, but avoidable, losses. They would just deduct what they understood, from Horizon, to be a loss from the Subpostmasters. One day, they returned a cheque presented by a customer at one of the branches as payment for an electricity bill. It had bounced. However, they paid the amount to the supplier, deducted the cash, and expected me to deal with it. I could not understand why they paid the supplier before the cheque cleared. Data protection and several other issues prevented us from being able to retrieve the money. Then there were the occasions when I noticed cheques that were sent to POL, but were not credited to us. After several conversations on the phone, they finally admitted their mistake and informed me that they would credit them back into my account. When I checked Horizon, I discovered that they had been debited instead. On yet another occasion, whilst I was leaving one of the branches, I found one of the special pouches we had handed to the Postman to deliver to Head Office, on the ground, outside the shop. It had all the documents, cheques, and reports within it. Had it not arrived to POL, I would have been liable and served an error and correction notices, demanding more money from me. I wonder how many other envelopes were mislaid, resulting in money being wrongly claimed from me, or others, for that matter?

Over a period of two years, I discussed and wrote about all these issues with the appropriate senior personnel from the group in an attempt to explain that there must have been something wrong with their system. On several occasions Horizon showed different results in the afternoon than was recorded in the morning. I discovered, during several gatherings with other Subpostmasters at POL communications events, that others had similar issues.

With so much money being deducted from remuneration, it had become financially critical. I needed to find other means of acquiring cash to keep the business going and staff employed. Cost savings in supplies and other expenditure were sought. Critical personal spending was made through a number of credit cards, overdrafts, and loans. It became clear that the best option was to offload the Post Offices by selling the branches to 'husband and wife' teams. I did not want the communities to lose the services we offer and, more importantly, put my staff out of work.

Then, to make matters worse, the Government decided that, as POL was making so many losses, cost savings must be made and over a 1000 Post Office branches need to close. To this end, POL carried out a study, which, after several months, identified my original West Beach branch as one of those that would close. A document was sent confirming this, along with the value of a compensation package, which, would be paid to Subpostmasters. I was to get just over £40,000 for the loss of the branch and its consequences. It was sad for those who relied on it. However, the other branch, which was less than a mile away, would be kept open, serving the community and employing staff. Also, this offered some respite for my increasing cashflow issues.

During the initial process, I could not find anyone who was interested in buying any of the branches. Understandably, no one would invest in something that might cease to exist. Adding to the problems were the signs of a looming recession. Suppliers started demanding substantial cash deposits before they would deliver; there was an immediate demand for £12,000 from the newspaper distributers, in order that deliveries may continue. Other suppliers insisted on cash with order, or on delivery. On the other hand, POL continued to demand money claimed as shortages. These unfair claims increased, whilst, at the same time, demands for large deposits, less favourable payment terms, high increases in labour and services costs, and caution from customers threatened every means of earnings. Despite continued protests, claims of system issues and pleas to the fact that they were forcing me into bankruptcy, POL would not relent. The compensation was delayed, even after the consultation period had ended. I had reached breaking point.

The cashflow continued to deteriorate, reaching a point where hard choices had to be made. Head Office was not willing to help, and I had to find a way to survive whilst keeping everyone happy. Obviously, I was strongly convinced that POL, through their dysfunctional system, had been and continued taking cash from me. Furthermore, despite the fact that they had over £40,000 in compensation owing to me, they refused to answer what had become real and serious cries for help. I was between a rock and a hard place, but I had to do something. Credits from banks had reached their limit and personal bankcards and other sources of finance were fully utilised. Cash was quickly drying up. I was on my own and had to find a way to deal with this.

If I had let an employee go and taken his or her place, I would become fixed to one location, with no time to carry out important operational activities. Also, the savings made would be minimal and someone would lose their livelihood, which I really wanted to avoid. I considered that if I were to secure a position for myself, elsewhere, it would probably pay more than my employee's costs. This, I believed, was the best option, providing necessary income, whilst allowing time for operational tasks, necessary for running the business.

I found a job at a local petrol station, working six evenings per week. After the shops and Post Offices shut, I started my shift, filling shelves, collecting money for petrol and goods, other purchases, and carry outgeneral duties, requested by the manager. After closure at 11p.m. I would switch and lock the petrol pumps, lock external cupboards, prepare newspaper returns, and mop the floors.

One of the tasks I was given was to ensure the public toilet is kept clean and supplied with necessary paper. This was something I had never had to do throughout my life and hated doing. It was made worse when, one day, I opened the toilet to find excrement everywhere. It was as if someone's stomach had exploded, spreading its contents in the bowl, on the walls and the floor. At that point, I was on the brink of breakdown, asking God what it was that I had done to deserve all this.

Following yet more unexplained error reports and demands for money, I was forced to write another letter to the Managing Director of POL, AC. In it, I had written that they had not been able to prove, beyond a shadow of a doubt, most of the errors, and had not supplied me with evidence, conclusive enough to counter my numerous disputes. I explained that the debts and payments during certain periods represented over 40% of the offices' remuneration. I stated that I was very happy to meet him, or an authorised representative who can help sort out the problem. His reply basically just reiterated previous communications and confirmed that there were no issues with their systems.

About a month later, I received yet a further error report stating that I owed POL, from the two remaining branches, £13,527, which must be settled immediately. I was beside myself and quickly called Head Office staff and wrote letters of disbelief, calling for a meeting to discuss the situation.

Written communications with the Agents Contracts Manager, regretfully, was not fruitful, necessitating further correspondence with senior personnel. Finally, there was some respite, in the form of a compromise, whereby POL would collect payment of the amount in instalments.

Despite all efforts, it became confirmed that there will be no possibility of them conceding to anything. For this business to continue, with its employees intact, cash must be found from any other source. Every possibility was blocked out to me. My bank overdrafts and loans were maxed out, credit cards were at their limits, and the money I was earning from the petrol station was barely enough to buy basic stock and pay for our household needs. The only way I could do this was to "borrow" the money from the £40,000 compensation, which was yet to be paid by POL. That is, the accounts had to be creatively presented. In order to protect them and me, I asked the assistants to document everything. When I needed an amount of cash urgently, to pay for utilities, stock, or wages, I would write a post-dated cheque, covering it. The dates of the cheques would coincide with an anticipated remuneration and income from the Post Offices and business. This was to prove to POL that I was not attempting to take money behind their back. The amounts would, also, pay for the demanded repayments of recent shortages and errors that kept coming. I knew that, once I received the money, it would more than cover any necessary borrowing and would, in a small way, compensate for the unfair claims by POL. This did not mean that I had accepted that the money taken by them as repayment for earlier shortages was justified. It was the best of all the options I had. My hope and belief was that I would receive the compensation money within three weeks, by the next remuneration payment.

Sadly, yet again, this did not happen. Payments required, had to be delayed as long as possible, and stock was minimised to the bare minimum. At least, we were plodding along as best we could. The employees had jobs and the community had a much-needed Post Office. I spent many sleepless nights, and, on some occasions, barely had enough money to buy a litre of petrol.

Finally, I met the Agents Contracts Manager and her assistant. There was a long and heated debate where the assistant was taking notes and no agreements, or movement forward were made. It was obvious all she wanted to do was to make me believe that it was entirely my fault. POL made it perfectly clear that the onus was on the Postmaster to prove his innocence. The meeting was finally concluded with no willingness from POL to admit that there was an error on their part, or to help me in anyway, except to continue to withdraw repayments for the debts in instalments. A couple of days later, I received the minutes of the meeting only to find huge inaccuracies, to say the least. Several pieces of information were taken in the wrong context and some important facts twisted or excluded. Following my angry reply to her, she sent a letter in which she accused me of mismanaging the branches and not checking to ensure correct processes were carried out and reports submitted properly. Basically, again, she was insisting that there were no problems with the Group's systems and that it was entirely my fault. She went on to say that I was causing POL losses due to the fact that they had to pay their clients, and my shortfall rendered them unable to do so. Several correspondences, including to more senior personnel followed, contesting what had been written and reiterating my poor financial position. I stated that, again, they were leading me into bankruptcy. I wondered if they ever considered the compensation due to me but not yet paid?

A Mean And Vindictive Blow

Two months later, on the 17th of March 2008, in the morning, I received a call from one of the branches, informing me that members of staff from POL were carrying out an unannounced audit. I called the other branch and heard that the same thing was happening there. Feeling anxious and panic, I quickly drove to the furthest branch to find out what was happening. They would not say anything; just that the Post Office would be closed for the next couple of days to assess shortages and accounting discrepancies. The same was happening in the other branch. In the late afternoon, following completion of the audits, I was accompanied to my house by two investigators, carrying notebooks, calculators, and empty boxes. They were to go through my house, searching for money, valuable items or any incriminating evidence.

I felt that I had nothing to hide, so allowed them to carry on. At the same time, I was scared, having heard that a couple of Postmasters had been prosecuted for shortages of money in their offices. I started thinking about the worst possible outcome, but I tried to remind myself that I had not done anything wrong. Everything was documented and clear. After all, they still have £40,000 of my money.

After hours of sifting through shelves, books, documents, drawers and anywhere that might lead to evidence of theft, they announced that they will be carrying out a recorded interrogation with me and asked if I would like anyone else to join us. Although, whilst searching, they, occasionally, looked at each other, implying that they had found incriminating evidence, I did not feel I was guilty of stealing anything and therefore declined. Nevertheless, it was nerve-wracking and very difficult to think straight, with a mind full of questions. "What is happening? Was I wrong?" and, "I am beaten and totally broken."

During the interview, I was as honest as possible and told them everything. They informed me that the total amount of the discrepancies for the two offices was over £50,000 and asked if I could pay this in full now. The figure sounded much higher than I imagined, and I could not immediately pay it. I explained that POL had just over £40,000 that should be given to me for the closure of the first branch. An hour later they stopped the recording and informed me that the person who would review this was not available for two weeks. However, I would be called to a disciplinary meeting to discuss this and the way forward. They collected two boxes of 'evidence' and left. The 'disciplinary' meeting never took place!

A few days later, I received a letter from the Contracts manager, formally confirming my suspension as Subpostmaster. I would not be allowed to run the Post Offices, my outstanding remunerations would be withheld and payment for that period would be determined by "contractual agreements." A company, who was endorsed by POL, was recommended to run the Post Offices, and I was urged to contact them quickly to expedite reopening them. I felt I had no other choice and accepted that company's terms of keeping any remuneration generated by the branches and only paying me a nominal amount for rental of the area and its utilities. They took over the offices and continued to run them for over a year. I received, on average, approximately £350 per month, instead of the about £3,500 average income.

The final results, detailing the shortages and amount owed to POL was prepared and sent to me in a document, at the end of the month. They had calculated that the total debt was £62,755. This included past outstanding debts identified as shortages up to the 9th of January, and was in fact, being withdrawn by instalments from remunerations. The compensation of £40,362 and unpaid remunerations of £2798 were deducted from the total, to arrive at the outstanding amount owed to them.

I could not question this and was sure that it was exaggerated and not calculated properly. However, fear and the inability of accessing the office forced me to accept it. The document they had sent was not easy to understand and did not write the net figure of the final debt, which I calculated to be £19,957. However, even though I had not operated the branches since the 17th of March, they had subsequently written to me with more 'shortages' that had been found.

I understood that there would be a two-week period before anything happened. This was opportune as, a year earlier, I had been nominated and asked to join a group of trainers to prepare and present a management-training program for the Egyptian Post Office (EPO). And, no, it had nothing to do with POL. EPO decided that, in order to develop and further grow, their managers had to be properly trained. A partnership from the UK, including me, was selected. Several training providers in Egypt, who knew me, my training ability, knowledge, and experience, suggested that I would be a valuable contributor to the programme. After a year's preparation, it was now time to deliver my weeklong part, in Cairo, commencing on the second week of April. The POL issues had to be forced to the back of my mind, so that I may conduct the course effectively and well. However, due to the circumstances, it turned out to be the longest week of my life. I could not stop thinking about how I may, not only be prosecuted, but, worse, go to prison, and how unfairly and harshly I had been treated.

In Cairo, a venue was prepared for us in a military club, which included a five-star hotel. Managers from all over Egypt were selected to attend the three-week course. The head of EPO and other senior managers met us and discussed the program. We confirmed to them the schedule of the course, which was to run over five days per week, starting from Sunday to Thursday at 9:00 a.m. and finishing at 5:00 p.m. It was set up with a bilingual communicating system, providing instantaneous translation from English to Arabic.

There were about 12 trainees at middle to senior management levels. As heads of major branches, they travelled from all regions of Egypt. EPO's major objective was to develop and provide the country with first class services and products, serving the population with excellence. To do this, they felt that their Heads must understand efficient, world-class management techniques and practice them to ensure success. A couple of very senior directors, also, attended a few of the sessions. Fortunately, I was able to communicate in both languages and felt it went very well. I had all but forgotten all about back home and its problems, albeit only during the daily sessions, until my departure date.

On my return to the UK, I was able to use the money earned from the training course to pay off critical debts. The money we needed to survive had to be borrowed from family. I was very short of cash and had more debts and outgoings than income, so was forced back to the petrol station to ensure the shops continued to operate with no loss of jobs. However, at times, I had no more than a couple of pounds in my pocket, which I used to put petrol in the car for the odd journey to purchase necessary stock and visit the shops. All the employees were paid from shop sales and by reducing the number of stock purchases to a bare minimum. Sales were impacted and I started being pulled down into a whirlpool. Little cash meant fewer stock items, reducing income, leading to even less cash.

A couple of months later, to my horror, I received a summons to appear at the local Magistrates Court. I was shaking as I opened it and read that POL had charged me with taking money from them and using it for my benefit, leaving them at risk of loss. My heart sank and I was shocked that they would do this, without giving me the chance to meet and discuss the situation. They never invited me to the usual 'disciplinary' meeting.

Devastated, I had to return to the firm of Solicitors found earlier and see if they could do anything. I, also, had to ask if I could get legal aid, as I had no cash left. After further discussions with them, they told me that a solicitor they wanted to allocate to me, declined. However, they would find someone else. I was stunned, thinking, "Is it so hopeless?" Then, they explained why.

About 18 months earlier, before cash had become so critical, a new member of staff had been hired at one of the branches. She had been given a one-week training course and, following another week's observation, proved to be capable of doing the necessary work. Three weeks later, after receiving her wages, she claimed to be feeling unwell and went home. We discovered a discrepancy, amounting to just over £300 and attempted to call her to find out, first how she was, and if she could contact me to discuss what happened. She did not return my calls. I wrote explaining that we needed to talk urgently about a matter with the Post Office. Three days later, there was still no contact. I decided to visit her at home. She did not open the door. Knowing that one of the other employees had her number, I asked her to call and persuade her to come in. However, she did not. Finally, I decided to write to her asking for an urgent phone call, if not face-to-face contact.

Another week passed and there continued to be no communications from her whatsoever. I sought help and, as there was money missing, and she reacted in this way, I was strongly advised to involve the police. At first, I was very reluctant, but her persistent lack of communication forced me to do so. My hope was that they would manage to facilitate our meeting, and all would be sorted out. I did not want to hurt, and definitely not prosecute her. A few days later, the police took matters into their own hands, interviewing me and confirming that they had been able to contact her. Several months later, they decided that there was a good case against her and decided to press charges.

It was this that caused the solicitor, originally nominated to represent me, to decline doing so. He had been representing the same employee whom I had to report to the police, for over a year. In fact, due to the charges against me, he managed to acquit her on the grounds that I was untrustworthy and may well have taken the money myself.

The solicitors asked me to attend several interviews to discuss POL's charges. At their request, I handed over all the documents

I had, which related to the incident and spent hours discussing events leading to the charges. During this time and in an attempt to persuade POL not to pursue litigation, I wrote to various people, including the Contracts Manager, and several senior personnel up to the head of Royal Mail. In my correspondences, I explained the situation and the issues leading to it. The question of the possible inaccuracies and malfunction of their systems, together with the constant insistence by POL that the shortfalls and debt are due solely to me, were raised. Also, the fact that following the audit, the actual shortfall stated, less the £40,000 due to me as compensation for closing the West Beach Office, left a net debt of just under £12,000. I further explained that the final figure, presented by them, included other unconfirmed shortfalls that, apparently, had come to light long after I had been suspended from running the offices. Also included were debts that had been identified to us, with an agreement reached for it to be paid off in instalments. This debt totalled £13,527, and £1,511 of it should have already been deducted from remunerations before the audit.

So, what are we talking about here? I tried to breakdown the 'final" figures submitted to me on the 26th of March 2008, revealing the figures below:

Shortfall calculated by the Audit team	£50,619
Total recent debt recorded by POL earlier and audits	£62,755
Compensation for office closure to be deducted	£40,363
Final remuneration for all offices to be deducted	£ 2,798
The amount owed to POL	£19594

It was not made clear whether or not that the final figure included the £1,511 that should have been collected from the January and February remunerations. If it had been deducted from the above amount owing, it would have left only £18083 outstanding. Even that amount could have been incorrectly calculated if, as I believed it to be, their system was malfunctioning, or due to including unsubstantiated shortfalls.

Cash availability became a nightmare. There were other assets, but they could not be touched and were out of my control. However, I managed to borrow, from family, £10,000 and paid it to POL. The result of this should have been an outstanding debt to be paid of just over £8,000 or £9,000. However, they informed me, months later, that errors had to be adjusted bringing the total now owing to £13,280. Despite protest and demands for proof of how this figure was derived, no reply was given. It looked very close to the final demand of £13, 500 agreed in January to be collected by instalments. Their figures and demands were unclear and full of discrepancies.

In my communications, I pleaded with them not to prosecute me over such a relatively small amount. I asked that they allow me to meet them to discuss and solve this without the need for litigation. I had never been in such a position, never had any litigation against me and that I was put between a rock and a hard place to keep the Post Offices open for the community and protecting employees' livelihood. Should I have been allowed to run the branches, with close control from POL, the so-called debt could have been collected within four months.

POL stated, in their summons, that I "…dishonestly made a false representation that you had deposited cheques…when you had not, intending to make a gain for yourself or expose the post office to a risk of loss." I could not understand this, as everything was documented, and post-dated cheques were left at the branches. I had explained to POL and solicitors that, to ensure transparency and proof of good intentions, protecting both them and myself, I wrote the cheques and left them in the safe to aid in the cash flow imbalance that I had been forced into. Deposited cheques were paid into the accounts on the due date when cash was received. This gesture of good intentions was used against me, in justifying the prosecution.

The results were always the same. They insisted that they did not have a problem with their systems; I have used public funds for my own benefit and left the Post Office at risk of loss. Their main objective was for me to pay back everything without a promise of not continuing with the prosecution and, apparently, maximising the chances of a custodial sentence.

I was informed that I was summoned to appear at Brighton Magistrates court in September. The solicitors informed me to plead guilty, at the earliest opportunity to reduce the risk of being physically imprisoned. Although they could see that I had no intention of dishonestly taking any money, they felt that something like this might be argued in a way to persuade a jury to find me guilty. Mitigating circumstances of actual events might have led to an acquittal, only if accepted. However, there was a high risk of this not happening. They drew up a 'Proof of Evidence' document, written in such a way as to confirm my guilt and substantiate it. I was told that it had to show, not only acknowledgement of the guilt, but, also, remorse.

Driven by the terror of being locked in a cell, I signed it. I was petrified and had no choice but to do as they suggested, even if I really did not believe that I should have even been prosecuted. Just being in this position, people started to judge me as a thief and definitely guilty. One person, my friend's partner, advised my wife to leave and distance herself from me. However, my wife, proving to be a much better person, denied her this pleasure. She believed in my innocence and good character, and stood by me.

Loufi and I met about 15 years earlier in Molesey, Surrey. She was a friend of my sister, who worked for an international oil company in Egypt and was on an assignment in the UK. I had been working abroad and had just returned for a couple of weeks. Snats had mentioned her, leaving me curious as to who this, seemingly, clever Egyptian woman is. Then, one day, whilst at home with Snats, Loufi arrived for a visit. As she entered, I could not help but think that she had surpassed my expectations. She was a beauty, with long wavy hair and big brown eyes. Her figure was the perfect hourglass, elegantly dressed and, obviously, a very successful lady. All I could say at the time was "Hi Loufi!" Apparently, at first, this did not resonate well with her.

We talked for a short while, and then sat with my brother, Sirkaak, to discuss printers, about which she had sought technical help. People mention that 'chemistry' determines the success of attractions between individuals. Judging by the sparks, which flew between us, I believe this to definitely be confirmed.

I found out that she was working at an office in a building, belonging to her company, in London overlooking the river Thames. The following day, I could not help myself and visited her there. The landmark building in which she worked was enormous, securely guarded and, towered over the Southbank of the river. She was informed of my presence and came down to collect me. The feelings I had the previous evening strengthened following the appearance of the mannequin who walked towards me. We spent a few minutes in her office on the twentieth floor, overlooking the Houses of Parliament on the west and St. Pauls, to the east, before heading to lunch in the large well-stocked restaurant in the basement of the building.

It transpired that she was separated from her husband and had a three-year-old daughter. She had been educated in private English-speaking schools, graduated from the AUC, and was exposed to several cultures, particularly the Dutch and British as well as, of course, Egyptian and other Arabs. She held the position of director on the Board of several subsidiaries of her company, and a Senior Manager within her division in Egypt. After several encounters, she made me feel whole and communication with her was stimulating. We were on the same wavelength, and she understood my work and, more importantly, the person I really am. I also loved her daughter, whom I describe as my own. I realised that God had sent me a beautiful family – an attractive, intelligent, and loving wife, and daughter.

After all these years, Loufi stood by me, believing in my innocence. My friend's wife was rebuked, confirming that I had been given the best, most supportive partner anyone could have. I would not be facing this horrible prosecution alone.

The day in court arrived and I was beside myself; I had lost the fight to prevent prosecution. In the building there were posters everywhere advising defendants to plead guilty at the earliest opportunity to reduce their sentence by up to 30%. There were notices from which one would know the time of sitting, together with the courtroom number in which the hearing is to take place. I went to the appropriate room and waited for the solicitor who would defend me.

Whilst waiting, I looked around at the people who were there and wondered how many of them should never have been summoned in the first place. I heard a lady talking to her lawyer about her council benefit's fraudulent claim. Another young man was charged with theft of articles from a company and a third who was charged with painting graffiti on a building. Although I did not know what to expect, I felt that I should not be there. I did not know the attorney who would represent me. When he arrived, we chatted about my case and the fact that I probably would not have to enter a plea at this time. It was a matter of appearing and confirming the charge and my details.

During another hearing, I knew that I had to plead guilty and had a statement describing my guilt and remorse presented to the courts. During the hearing, it was decided that my charges were serious enough, due to the high value of the shortages found as a result of the audit, to warrant a trial by the Crown Court. The Magistrates ruled that this should happen and that the solicitors would have to present all the appropriate paperwork at a final hearing to commit me to the higher court. On the day of that hearing, the Post Office prosecuting council asked for a two-week extension. To my surprise, the magistrates decided not to grant them this and dismissed the case. However, if they wanted to, POL was allowed to restart the process from scratch. My solicitor informed me that the Post Office team would see this as "a punch on the nose." They would, therefore, be unlikely to want to return. He went on to say, "You're free!"

I felt like the whole world was lifted off my shoulders. I was so happy, my eyes started to water, and the feeling of relief passed through my body like water, falling from mountaintops, forms a river along a valley. I couldn't wait to meet my wife and tell her this great news. Perhaps now, I could carry on with the rest of my life.

The Bully Must Have Her Pound of Flesh

One of the things I had to do before the court appearance was to try and save the very badly damaged and struggling business. I visited a shopkeeper who, along with his wife and child, owned a convenience store near Mill Lane. After several discussions, I persuaded them to buy the Mill Lane shop and Post Office. My proposal was that they pay me for the stock and, through an intermediate contract, run the business as if it was their own. That meant, they pay all the expenses and keep the profits. Due to my extremely poor cash flow situation, this would ensure the continuation and survival of the entity. The contract allowed them six months before they must have completed the purchase at the agreed price. The Post Offices continued to be run by the POL's recommended company.

In order to maintain the Post Office operations within the shop, the prospective buyer's wife had to apply to POL to become a Subposmistress, and be accepted. This proved difficult, as she was not confident that she would get it. I knew that I could not lose them, whilst, at the same time, ensure they moved forward with the purchase process without delay. Of course, they also tried to reduce the price further; already they were getting it for £40,000 less than the original asking price.

The other branch, East Beach, also, had a prospective buyer who, knowing about my predicament with POL and my lack of cash and desperation, drove the price down to virtually 40% of its value. He was, also, dragging his feet and felt unsure about taking on the Post Office part of the business. Making matters worse, the landlady had to accept the potential buyer. Although the gentleman, originally from Turkey, appeared well mannered, honest, and capable, it took her several months to be persuaded to accept him. If the shop was not sold, I would have had no option but to close it. Had this happened, employees would become unemployed, the Post Office would be gone, and, with the recession looming, she would lose her rental income.

The great financial recession of 2008 was taking its toll. There were very few, if any, buyers. As I waited for someone to brave this dreadful calamity and buy the business, I had to earn more money to keep it from collapsing. The vultures at Mill Lane and East Beach were waiting for me to go to prison, leaving the businesses to them for a fraction of its worth.

Now that the case brought about by POL was thrown out, I visited them, asserting my freedom and pushing for immediate completion. I managed to persuade the wife at Mill Lane to expedite her application to POL. Also, I found others who were interested and made sure they went to visit the shop so that the Sing family might fear that the business may be lost. Fortunately, they reacted positively and progressed their purchase and application to the Post Office.

In parallel with this, I had, applied to a company for a position as Training Advisor. Success, not only guaranteed more, much needed, income, but also being able to stop working for the petrol station. Following a period of induction and training at head office, I was ready to start the role, which, fortunately, was home based.

I was in total control of my time, making my own appointments and ensuring that each trainee/apprentice is visited at least once every two weeks. Within a couple of months I had a caseload of forty apprentices, whom I got on well with and supported until they met their targeted level. Sadly, the majority of trainees were very poor at mathematics. This prompted me to devise a course which would help them understand the subject whilst also enjoying it. The success of its execution led me to thinking about passing this and my knowledge and experiences to the younger generation. Although I had devised and delivered training programs to managers and employees, I felt a teaching qualification would be crucial; something to seriously consider in a few years' time.

Three months later, I was getting on with everyone and always helping where needed. My work and reputation was extremely good and invariably commented upon by my superiors and the companies in which I taught and assessed. I was travelling around the Southeast and seeing apprentices in organisations including retail, law firms, estate agents, and social aid providers. I loved it. Then, one day, out of the blue, another summons from POL arrived on my doorstep!

My solicitors had predicted this would not happen. Also, according to their final demand, I only owed POL the contested £13,300 pounds, which I promised to pay as soon as the business was sold. I was furious, scared and could not understand why they could not just meet with me and sort this out once and for all. Although my Post Offices were not under my control, they were operational. Further correspondences with POL's most senior personnel did not achieve anything.

They asked me to get a solicitor to write that they would be paid the money owed to them when the business was sold. However, they reiterated, "… the court case would have to run its course." I was also no nearer to completing any sale, continued to be in huge debt, and could not lose more money for solicitors to write further letters and complicate things. Further guarantee of any debt repayment to POL was available in the original contract between us. They could demand payment, from the solicitor handling the sale prior to confirming the new recipient's acceptance, or transferring the branches. I could not conclude any sale, nor get a penny, before this happened. So, had they thought about it properly, or wished to, they would have known that their money was already guaranteed. There was no need of continuing the prosecution.

Another visit to the Magistrates court led to my committal to a trial by the Crown Court. A custodial sentence was not out of the question, despite a guilty plea at the earliest opportunity. Of course, I had to tell my employers about what had happened, expecting to be dismissed. Fortunately, to my surprise, they said that, knowing me as they did, they could not believe this. "In the short time that you have worked with us, you have proved to be an honest reliable man who did not deserve this litigation," they said. As far as they were concerned, they wanted me to continue, unless, of course, I actually went to prison, and this, they felt, should not happen.

Although I was happy with their attitude, I knew POL would not help me. My last hope, I thought, was to write to the then Prime Minister, Gordon Brown, explaining the situation and events to date. I explained the situation and asked if he would help prevent me from going to prison, as I had to plead guilty to reduce the chances of this happening. The case was about a month away, leaving little time. However, I received a letter from his office informing me that he had asked the appropriate departments to investigate and handle this.

The first sitting at the Crown Court was straightforward, as I had pleaded guilty. The barrister representing me had only met me for the first time on the day and did not strive to use mitigating circumstances or attempt to acquit me. The judge asked that I attend with the Probationary Services in order for them to assess my situation, and me, and recommend a sentence. The sentencing trial was set for a month later.

Not a minute went by without me thinking about my dilemma. I was convinced that this was unfair and vindictive from the Contracts Manager's side. She had not kept it a secret how angry she had been that I had claimed that she basically lied in her reporting of our earlier meeting. Her report had been documented to paint a different picture to that which I actually presented. It seemed that she, through POL, had to get her pound of flesh.

Perhaps, the Judge would have realised the inappropriateness of the litigation when informed of the money POL owed me, and had in their possession, prior to the audit. The small value that had actually been outstanding and the events leading to the summons, may have swayed judgement. Having visited the probation offices, I could not recognise myself with the majority of the other defendants there. I kept thinking, "I am not a criminal," but had been forced to say I was to keep myself out of prison. I held positions controlling hundreds of millions of pounds and never even thought of diverting any of it to me. Although offered over a million pounds in 'bribes', I refused to accept them and ensured the organisations in which I worked benefited from them instead. I ran behind Post Office and store customers because they forgot or overpaid even a fraction of a pound. Furthermore, had POL seen the small value actually owed and allowed me, with a reprimand, and close monitoring, to run my Post Offices, they could have more than realised their demanded shortfalls. I had lost over £90,000 in revenue alone and lost sales during the 18 months until the final court case.

During the meeting and assessment with the Probationary officer, I was asked about my background, experiences, and qualifications and what I felt had happened with POL to lead to this. She was very supportive and appeared sympathetic, implying she could not see how it could have ended like this. She would write her report and recommendations before sending it to the judge for his decision.

On the day of the sentencing hearing, I arrived with my wife, mother-in-law, brother, Sirkaak, and sister-in-law. We were a bit earlier than the hearing to allow time to find out where we were supposed to go and to meet the new Barrister who would represent me. After we settled in the designated waiting area, the Barrister arrived, introduced himself and asked that both him and I should sit in a quiet area to talk about the case.

I had never seen him before and, it became obvious that he knew very little about me, and the background of my case. For only ten minutes, he was asking me about what happened and what I believe went wrong. After taking some notes, he explained the process during the proceedings and that my family would sit in an area next to 'the dock' in which I will stand for the duration of the sentencing. Before long, we were called by the usher to go into the courtroom.

I was led into the defendant's area in the middle of which was a staircase leading down. Should the judge pronounce a custodial sentence, I would be led down the stairs into a cell to wait for transport to prison – I guess that is where the phrase, "you're going down" came from. I was so frightened and consumed with images of my wife and family having to go back home without me. Indeed, I had given my wallet and phone to Loufi to take with her, should I be imprisoned. There was a guard who also stood in the dock on the side where we entered. I guess his presence was to ensure I did not escape. My Barrister sat diagonally to the left and further down and the POL prosecutors to the right. A local newspaper reporter sat on a bench to the side of the court and there were a few others attending. Then, the usher shouted, "all rise", allowing the judge to enter and sit behind his bench at the front of the court, opposite me. I had to remain standing while the others sat down.

During the proceedings, my Barrister basically used the notes he took earlier to try and defend me. He seemed to be struggling and did not mention any of the things I thought might have shown enough mitigating circumstances leading to, I dared to hope, perhaps, an acquittal. No mention was made of the £40,000 that was in POL's possession when they audited the offices, the fact that all the outstanding money had been paid and, more importantly, the claim that POL's system may have been inaccurate. He continued to talk about reasons including, the recession, which the judge did not accept.

References concerning me had been requested from three people, who knew me well, and given to the judge prior to the sentencing hearing. One of the references was written by a dear friend who was a respectable Doctor (PhD) working in a very senior position, for a company that dealt with the ministry of defence. David, in his letter, stated that he always saw me as a respectable, honest and law-abiding citizen. He criticized POL for the way they treated me, their lack of understanding and total denial that the fault may well have been due to their Horizon system. Having read this, the judge was angry, waving the reference, criticizing the author and proclaiming that he would not accept it! Obviously, I thought, the judge had already made up his mind of my guilt and POL's correct decision to have me punished. I prepared myself for the worst possible outcome.

As my Barrister continued with his poor attempt at defending me, a person walked into the court, up to the front bench and handed a folded note to the Judge. After reading it the judge stopped the Barrister from continuing, saying, "I will put you out of your misery." He started to summarise the hearing and before pronouncing the sentence, looked at me and said, "…until now you had been a gentleman of good character. You will no longer be seen as that…"

He informed me that the maximum sentence I could get for such a crime could be up to six years in jail. However, as I had pleaded guilty at the earliest opportunity and have, until now, been of good character with no previous convictions, he would be lenient. The sentence he pronounced was a custodial one, lasting for 52 weeks for each of the two charges, running concurrently. My heart sank and I could hardly stand. I was utterly shocked and terrified that I would be 'going down.'

The judge went on to say that he would suspend this sentence for two years and included 180 hours of non-paid work (Community Service). I felt as if all the earth that had been shovelled on top of me was lifted away. I did not have to go to prison! My wife and family were incredibly happy. So much so, that my mother-in-law walked up to the Barrister, gave him a kiss on the cheek and whispered "Thank you."

The ordeal, with its huge stress and uncertainty, had passed. However, my nightmares had just begun. Not a single hour of a single day passed when I did not think about what I had been put through and the unfairness of it all. I am trapped in an endless playback constantly in my mind.

A Deep Dark Empty Hole

There were several consequences of the conviction; one example was the home insurance due for renewal. A question asked on the renewal form was, "have you, or any member of your household, ever been convicted..." It dawned on me that, now, I have what I believed could never have been given to me, a criminal record. I was refused insurance, with others trebling their costs, and debts were coming out of my ears. I had to push the prospective buyers of the businesses to conclude the purchase. Whereas in the past, they had been waiting for me to be locked up, to get everything for free, they now had to pay or lose it. They had plenty of time to see, and experience, the huge potential of the shops. However, it would be many months before any cash would be realised and cashflow, one of business's main lifeline, was being decimated. Fortunately, my job carried on and I was earning enough to just survive.

I had to undertake the 180 hours of unpaid work. However, as a fulltime employee, it would be difficult to do. My allocated probation officer was understanding and found me a suitable post. I worked on a Saturday and Sunday in a furniture charity shop, ten minutes' walk from where I lived. It was as if I, as most of the workers there, volunteered. Unlike other community workers, I did not have to be outside in all weather and did not have to wear the Hi-Viz jacket labelled to show the wearer was completing a punishment set by the court.

The people I worked with were friendly, helpful, loyal, and reliable. As far as I was concerned, I had to be there. However,

I was, also, helping the needy and other charitable institutions. Very quickly, I was trusted enough to be left on my own to look after the premises, sell goods and accept cash. I, also, had to carry out mundane jobs like washing kitchenware, rearranging furniture, and cleaning floors.

Sadly, I could not stop thinking about the Post Office and their unfair, inhumane treatment of me. The events leading to the predicament in which I find myself, kept playing in my mind, like a movie that was stuck in a loop. In the evenings, when I got into bed, making it very difficult to sleep and, when I eventually manage to sleep, it wakes me very early the following morning. These scenarios continued throughout the day.

How can any organisation, in this case a government one, be so resistant to acknowledging fault, so uncaring about its franchisees and so vindictive that, I believe, allows personal feelings to destroy a person or family. The reason I consider this, is because if they were caring, they would have seen that there was no real 'risk of loss' when the net amount of shortfall was shown to be a quarter of the audited value. Also, they had known me for over five years and must have realised that I am not that type of person. Had they allowed me to retake control of the offices, any shortfall could have been paid back quickly. It seems, perhaps, that all the Contracts Manager thought about was, "I will get him." Even the most senior person appeared to have been led by his subordinates alone, despite knowing the damage the action would cause. The litigation alone must have cost tax-payers tens or even hundreds of thousands of pounds. But they did not seem to care about that.

Royal Mail claimed that I had left them with a risk of loss amounting to just over £50,000. Yet earlier, despite their supposedly well-qualified and experienced managers, it was reported that POL had lost approximately £208 million in 2006/2007. These were actual losses, caused by the way they ran the business, and their decision making, rather than just a "risk of loss", which they claimed in the charges raised against me. Probably, mismanagement, mistakes and inefficiencies caused a great deal of these. Perhaps, system faults digitally generated the losses, which were passed onto the unsuspecting Subpostmasters. Despite their enormous losses, POL's Managing Director was due to be given a £1 million bonus!

I had written to him, begging not to have my life destroyed over a contested £13,000. His only reply was to let the courts take their normal course. The giant gets a million pounds, when the company he managed lost over £200 million of public funds. Little me had to be destroyed for an uncertain 0.006% of that amount!

Creditors started chasing me with demands for repayments of the debts. At that point, apart from the sizeable mortgage, my debts amounted to over £200,000. Calls and notices from County Courts started to appear with 'judgments' pronounced against me. Bailiffs threatened to come to my house and take any valuables to pay money owed. I started hating the ringtone of my phone, as it meant a creditor would be at the other end. I was worried, leaving home, or returning to it, lest there was someone waiting to grab me and force me to let him in to collect whatever he wants. I needed help; but there was no money!

There were companies that would help in dealing with creditors to reduce or renegotiate the instalments. Unfortunately, they charged a hefty fee for doing so. This led me to the Citizens Advise Bureau (CAB), where a volunteer, experienced in this sort of issue, could help. He advised me to first, and foremost, open a bank account, as this would not be possible after the credit report is updated. We worked together to compile a personal financial statement and explained that I should write to my creditors – of which there were 12 – explaining my predicament and asking them to, initially, stop charging interest on my debts. We had worked out the most I could afford, which was practically negligible, and divided it, proportionally, amongst them, to be paid monthly. Apparently, the recession, which was very severe, had affected many people, causing the Government to intervene to protect those affected from losing their homes and intimidation.

Most of the debts were related to the limited company I had set up. However, the financing necessary for the activities, including banking loans and overdrafts and rents, had to be personally guaranteed by me. This meant that, even if the company was not performing well, or closed down, I would be liable for its debts. £100,000 of the debts, taken out to assist in the purchase of Mill Lane, was secured against our home. If I could not repay it, the bank could force me to sell the house to redeem the outstanding balance.

After several correspondences with the 12 creditors, I was able to reach agreements, allowing affordable instalment payments. Three of the creditors decided to take out a county court judgement against me. One of these was from the landlord of the original premises, who had threatened to do so, three months earlier. I had paid him a third of the amount outstanding and asked him to give me more time to pay the rest in two instalments. He continued to submit the claim with the original value of the debt, forcing me to attend a hearing. When I went for the hearing at the county court, he had not bothered to turn up.

I met with the judge dealing with the case, explained the situation and told her that I had already paid a third of the amount. Although the claimant was not present, and the amount demanded was wrong, she upheld the demand and informed me that I could apply to the courts again to appeal, or request repayment by instalments. It felt as if everyone was against me. Once you are down, everyone sees you as dishonest and not worthy of any compassion. Until then, I understood that a judge represents an unbiased person who attempts to fully understand the issues and pronounce the fairest judgement, taking account of all mitigating circumstances. From my experience, I am left to believe this not to be so, and that they may be guilty of stereotyping.

The type of person I am is most certainly not a fraudster, or worst, a thief. My background, work, life experiences and actions reflected this. My hope, and expectation, was that the individuals whose responsibility it is to decide one's future should take this into consideration. However, when the judge at the Crown Court read an honest reference about me, with views that the defendant is almost certain not to have knowingly committed a criminal offence and that the claimants are likely to have made a mistake, he showed a biased view. He was angry and refused to accept, or entertain the possibility that, perhaps, I was not guilty.

Previously, I had been asked to change my name to stand a better chance of getting an interview for a good job. I now find myself asking, had I agreed and changed my name, would things have turned out differently? Would the judge that ruled against me, have seen my actions and me in a better light?

Although I was very relieved that I was not physically imprisoned, my view of the position in which I find myself is on the floor of a deep, dark empty well. The way out of it to daylight seemed impossible. Throughout my life, I enjoyed the sunshine; offered by a good upbringing, alert mind, hard work and persistence. Despite obstacles and setbacks, I had always sought ways to move forward and progress.

Looking back at the person who is uncovered within the pages of this book, how would you judge him? Was POL correct and fair in its insistence? Was the attempt to save the business, maintaining the much-needed Post Offices for the community and saving employees' livelihood against a colossal entity, which denies any faults, but continues to inflict pain, a sign of guilt?

After five years of interaction with me, perhaps, POL could have shown more consideration and offered a face-to-face meeting to discuss what had happened and reach a win-win solution. Also, had they allowed me to continue control and running of the Post Offices and receipt of full remunerations, all outstanding amounts would have been recouped within four months. They would not have needed to spend taxpayers' money for the sole benefit of destroying an otherwise honest man. It would appear that the responsible personnel enjoyed inflicting humiliation, pain and suffering onto me and my family, whilst continuing with their day-to-day life, oblivious or uncaring of any consequences or costs.

Ahead of me, the future is unknown. What will the next ten years bring? Can I survive them? Could I find strength to get out of this abyss? But for now, having walked the path I travelled, lived my happiness, sorrow, doubts, fears, and pain, I ask you to **judge me if you can**.

╌╌╌╌ FÜR AUTOREN A HEART FOR AUTHORS À L'ÉCOUTE DES AUTEURS MIA KAPΔIA ГIA ΣΥΓΓ
╌╌╌╌ FÖR FÖRFATTARE UN CORAZÓN POR LOS AUTORES YAZARLARIMIZA GÖNÜL VERELIM SZ
╌╌╌╌ PER AUTORI ET HJERTE FOR FORFATTERE EEN HART VOOR SCHRIJVERS TEMOS OS AUT
╌╌╌╌ SERCE DLA AUTORÓW EIN HERZ FÜR AUTOREN A HEART FOR AUTHORS À L'ÉCO
╌╌╌╌ ВСЕЙ ДУШОЙ К АВТОРАМ ETT HJÄRTA FÖR FÖRFATTARE Á LA ESCUCHA DE LOS AUTO
╌╌╌╌ MIA KAPΔIA ГIA ΣΥΓΓΡΑΦΕΙΣ UN CUORE PER AUTORI ET HJERTE FOR FORFATTERE EEN

The author

Born in Cairo in 1955 to a medical doctor father and supporting mother, Sami Sabet lived an international life, being raised and educated in Egypt, Saudi Arabia, the US, Libya and England.

He holds an honour's degree in Electronics Engineering, a Master's in Business Administration (MBA) and a Post Graduate Certificate in Education (PGCE). Further qualifications include a Coaching Diploma from The Coaching Academy and accreditation in personality profiling.

His career began as an engineer in the UK, working for Philips Electronics and Gillette. Post MBA, Sami moved into Finance, Sales and Marketing and General Management. He, also, worked in Saudi Arabia, the US, North Africa, the Middle East and the Indian Subcontinent. This reinforced his exposure and understanding of lives and cultures across the globe, resulting in the devotion of his later life to helping others by teaching, lecturing, training and coaching.